"Russ Ramsey is a kind of songwriter of prose. The lyrical nature of his writing makes his Bible teaching memorable, accessible, and evocative. This volume will help you to understand and explain the story of our church through the book of Acts. It will also prompt you to love Acts and Jesus all the more."

Russell Moore, president of the Ethics & Religious Liberty Commission, author of *Onward: Engaging the Culture Without Losing the Gospel*

"Russ Ramsey has this lovely, compelling way of helping us see and savor Christ in all of Scripture. If you want to grow in your knowledge of the Bible, to be swept up into the grand story that it tells, and to see how it gives meaning to both your story and our story, then let *The Mission of the Body of Christ* be a mentor and companion in this quest. I can't recommend it highly enough."

Scott Sauls, senior pastor of Christ Presbyterian Church, author of *Jesus Outside the Lines* and *Befriend*

"Russ Ramsey is a wonderful storyteller, and in *The Mission of the Body of Christ* he weaves together bits from the Old Testament and the Gospels with the Acts of the Apostles and the Epistles to create a beautiful tapestry that imaginatively depicts the early days of the church. The gospel shines brightly in the pages of this book and the story of the gospel's impact on the world is told in the most engaging and enjoyable way I have ever read."

Ned Bustard, creative director of Square Halo Books, author of *Revealed: A Storybook Bible for Grown-Ups*

"With the voice of a storyteller and the affection of a pastor, Russ Ramsey brings the story of the early church to life in the present. With each character and scene, these pages provide a doorway for us to walk inside the narrative, inviting us to hear Paul's journey in a fresh way as we contemplate our own questions of faith."

Sandra McCracken, singer and songwriter, *Songs from the Valley, Psalms, Desire like Dynamite*

"Russ Ramsey's gift for retelling the stories of Scripture is second to none. This is as evident in everyday conversation with Russ as it is in his writing. I have never met an individual who loves Scripture more than this brother, and I am thankful to God for the gift of Russ and his books to the church."

Amanda Bible Williams, cofounder and chief content officer of She Reads Truth, He Reads Truth, and Kids Read Truth

"The best gift (among many) that Russ Ramsey offers the body of Christ is the gift of greater context. His writings have the power to lift readers from their present surroundings and set them down amid the clamoring, bustling, peopled streets of the ancient world. Ramsey's deep biblical knowledge and disciplined imagination serve to gently illuminate oft-overlooked nuances of culture, custom, and language, thereby allowing readers to experience these old stories as if for the first time."

Douglas McKelvey, author of *Every Moment Holy: New Liturgies for Everyday Life*

"The church isn't always a welcoming place for single women in their forties (like me). But the New Testament church is radically hospitable—a place for witness, unity, and love. *The Mission of the Body of Christ* is a vital contribution to this conversation. Salvation, after all, is a community-creating event. As Russ writes, 'The risen Jesus not only gave his people new life, he gave them each other.' And I'm thankful for that."

Bethany Jenkins, vice president of forums and content for the Veritas Forum

"For those of us church folk who are overly familiar with the Bible, it's easy to forget (or maybe we never learned) the richness of Scripture's narrative. For those new to faith in Jesus, the Bible can overwhelm and the story of redemption, mission, and transformation gets easily lost. Russ seeks to be a 'faithful servant of Scripture' and is he ever. His retelling of the Bible's stories doesn't distract—it amplifies. This book draws the reader into God's transforming word and does so with the craft of an artist and a pastor's soul. I cannot recommend *The Mission of the Body of Christ* enough."

Barnabas Piper, author and podcaster

"Russ is a modern-day scribe, taking his cues from the words of Scripture to reimagine stories, narratives, and scenes for his readers. He doesn't embellish or exaggerate. He tells and retells familiar narratives with a new perspective. Ordinary Christians living ordinary lives need *The Mission of the Body of Christ*, which is written to be read during ordinary time. We need to reimagine, relive, and see God's mission for the church afresh, to be reminded there is nothing ordinary about the story in which we live. Russ does this beautifully as always."

Lore Ferguson Wilbert, writer and speaker

RETELLING THE STORY SERIES

THE MISSION
OF THE
BODY OF CHRIST

RUSS RAMSEY

IVP Books

An imprint of InterVarsity Press
Downers Grove, Illinois

InterVarsity Press
P.O. Box 1400, Downers Grove, IL 60515-1426
ivpress.com
email@ivpress.com

InterVarsity Press is the book-publishing division of InterVarsity Christian Fellowship/USA, a movement of students and faculty active on campus at hundreds of universities, colleges, and schools of nursing in the United States of America, and a member movement of the International Fellowship of Evangelical Students. For information about local and regional activities, visit intervarsity.org.

Scripture quotations, unless otherwise noted, are from The Holy Bible, English Standard Version, copyright © 2001 by Crossway Bibles, a division of Good News Publishers. Used by permission. All rights reserved.

Published in association with the literary agency of Wolgemuth & Associates.

Cover design and illustration: David Fassett
Interior design: Jeanna Wiggins

ISBN 978-0-8308-4400-5 (print)
ISBN 978-0-8308-8527-5 (digital)

Printed in the United States of America ∞

Library of Congress Cataloging-in-Publication Data
A catalog record for this book is available from the Library of Congress.

| P | 20 | 19 | 18 | 17 | 16 | 15 | 14 | 13 | 12 | 11 | 10 | 9 | 8 | 7 | 6 | 5 | 4 | 3 | 2 | 1 |
| Y | 35 | 34 | 33 | 32 | 31 | 30 | 29 | 28 | 27 | 26 | 25 | 24 | 23 | 22 | 21 | 20 | 19 | 18 |

FOR RYAN, my brother.

I am so thankful our roots

are deep in the soil of

the church and that I got

to grow up with you.

CONTENTS

PART 3: THE MISSIONARY JOURNEYS, AD 46–57

PART 4: ROME AND BEYOND, AD 57–62

PREFACE

I WANT PEOPLE TO KNOW WHAT THE BIBLE SAYS. The details in the pages of Scripture tell a riveting story. Since the Bible was not written during a time when reams of paper and junk drawers full of pens were readily available, we can trust that Scripture was written in thrift. The details on the page are there to help us see things we might have missed otherwise.

For the first two books in this Retelling the Story series, I covered quite a range of biblical text: the entire Old Testament in twenty-five chapters for *The Advent of the Lamb of God,* and a forty-chapter synthesis of the four Gospels for *The Passion of the King of Glory.* This book, *The Mission of the Body of Christ,* presented a different challenge. It centers on a single biblical book, the Acts of the Apostles, but also draws from the narrative details peppered throughout the New Testament Epistles.

It is not always clear how the Epistles' references to people and events connect to the timeline in Acts. Before I wrote a word of this book, I created some spreadsheets in an attempt to map out the events of the book of Acts. I wanted to get a bird's eye view of what happened, when, and to whom. I wanted to see how Paul's missionary journeys lined up with the letters he wrote. I wanted to follow the story on a map. I wanted to try to keep track of characters who stepped in and out of the story along the way. I wanted to understand the passage of time. So I charted as much of this as I could, with as much certainty as I could, based on my own study of Scripture and scholarly works.

I did not write *The Mission of the Body of Christ* to be a substitute for reading the Bible. I want this book to serve as a faithful servant of Scripture. I've included hundreds of Scripture references in this manuscript. Let me explain why. Throughout this book I paraphrase in order to maintain a unified voice. Rarely do I quote Scripture directly or at length. This applies to dialogue as well. If a character says something and there's a Scripture reference attached in the endnotes, that doesn't necessarily mean I'm quoting the original text. I'm probably not. More than likely I'm paraphrasing and distilling a larger moment in Scripture to work within the scope of this book. The references I include are there to lead you to the stories Scripture unfolds with perfect sufficiency.

While I'm on this point, I should note that I engage in some speculation in this book—imagining how certain conversations happened, how particular characters felt, and what various scenes looked like. I have tried to limit my speculations to reasonable inferences that wouldn't redirect the Bible's narrative arc. I've avoided inventing characters or manufacturing extrabiblical encounters. I have tried to keep my speculative input within the natural and plausible lines of human nature.

The story told in these pages is my story. Every picture of brokenness is in some measure the story of my own brokenness. Every need that rises to the surface is in some way a need I share. Every tendency toward rebellion, every cry of desperation, every prayer for forgiveness, and every hope of redemption rings true in me. I do not write as a removed researcher. I write as an eyewitness to the impact this story has had on my own life and the world I inhabit.

Thank you for reading. To give my life to the study and expression of Scripture is one of my greatest joys. As a pastor, cultivating biblical literacy is one of my most important goals. My highest hope for this book is that it will deepen your understanding of the wonder and glory of the story of the Bible.

PART 1

JERUSALEM

AD 30–33

1

A LETTER FROM
AN OLD FRIEND

Philemon 1-25

*T*HE SERVANT WHO ANSWERED THE DOOR wore a look of disbelief. The last person she expected to find when she heard the knock was Onesimus, who stood there with his traveling companion Tychicus.

Tychicus was the first to speak. "Please tell the master of the house that we come bearing letters from the apostle Paul, who is in Rome. One is for the church that meets in this house. The other is for him personally; it concerns my brother Onesimus here."

The servant looked at the letters in Onesimus's hands and ran off to find Philemon.

Years earlier, Onesimus had been a slave in the city of Colossae. As such he'd had a tough life. But when he ran away to Rome it got even tougher. Colossae and Rome were twelve hundred miles apart.

The only means he had to traverse that distance were boats, horses, and his own two feet.

Onesimus was Philemon's slave. Slavery was essential to Rome's social order. The entire empire was built on the backs of slaves owned by "men of nobility" who believed it was beneath them to work. Though some slaves in Rome may have had kind masters, the reality was that slaves were still property with no rights or protection. Onesimus wanted out.

When Onesimus committed to his escape, he arranged some basic preparations: money for the road and belongings to disguise the fact that he was a runaway. These he took from Philemon. He knew the minute he stepped out on his own he was in trouble. Stealing from his master was a capital crime for slaves in Rome. This wasn't an uncommon practice, however. To escape meant to risk facing the wrath of the slaveholder anyway, so many who fled also stole from their masters on their way out in the hopes of funding a clean getaway.

But fleeing their current situation usually meant stepping into one that was worse. Since a flight like Onesimus's would have been close to impossible without help, he had to become part of the underworld of runaway slaves and criminals. He entered a society of fugitives evading arrest. Since there is no honor among thieves, this was a notoriously dangerous network to tangle with.

Along with dangers within, there were dangers without. Historically, for every society of fugitives seeking to stay underground there has been a countersociety of bounty hunters who make their living hunting them down and handing them back over for a reward. Onesimus was in trouble because runaway slaves were the bounty hunters' bread and butter—easy to find because they lacked the necessary means to purchase anonymity. This was the world

Onesimus entered when he ran—a world of fugitives, stowaways, thieves, criminals, and bounty hunters looking to get paid. A large, diverse city like Rome was the perfect place to disappear. Many went there to do just that. With Colossae at his back, Onesimus set his face to the Eternal City. He paid smugglers for passage, made up stories to hitch rides, and changed his appearance often to blend in. He lived every one of those days looking over his shoulder. When he finally arrived in Rome, the hope of a new beginning rose inside him. Now he just had to figure out a way to make his lie his truth.

Having divided his years between being a slave and being a fugitive, Onesimus had plenty of time to ask why his life had become what it had. He would not have wished his plight on anyone. But in his heart raged a protest. He was not meant to be another man's slave. He was not meant to be known as the property of another. He was not a commodity. He was a man. He didn't choose to be born into his low position. Part of the reason he had run away was that he objected to being reduced to something so insignificant. He might die as a fugitive, but at least it would be on his own terms.

Onesimus's position softened a bit when his money ran out. Except for the company of thieves, he found himself alone in Rome—and broke. Like the prodigal son who blew through his father's inheritance, Onesimus began to shift from dreams of independence to a desperate need for help. In this underground world he was vulnerable. He needed to find safety.

He had heard there was a man in Rome named Paul, the apostle who'd led his master Philemon to faith in Jesus of Nazareth. Onesimus knew Paul was a man who specialized in helping people who were lost. He had seen firsthand the transformation of many people's lives through the church that met in Philemon's home. When people heard Paul's gospel, something in them seemed to shake free. Peace and joy took the place of cynicism and contempt. When Onesimus learned the apostle was a prisoner under house arrest, he sought him out. Perhaps they could help each other, he thought.

Onesimus found Paul and told him parts of his story, but whatever thoughts he had about trading favors with the prisoner soon vanished when the old apostle told the runaway slave about Jesus. Paul spoke with an uncommon conviction—like he was prepared to die proclaiming the message of salvation by grace through faith in the life, death, and resurrection of the man from Nazareth.

Onesimus heard this gospel and put his faith in the same Lord his master had. It wasn't so much that Onesimus took hold of Christ. It was that Christ took hold of him. Onesimus attended to Paul like a son attended to an aging father, and Paul loved him as his own child.

Soon Onesimus began to struggle with what to do about his broken relationship with Philemon. His faith had an ethic. Though he had plenty of reasons to justify running away—reasons that, in turn, justified his thievery—he knew that because he and Philemon were both followers of Christ, they could not leave this fracture between them unaddressed.

Onesimus eventually told Paul the whole truth about what had happened and how he had come to Rome. He wanted to be reconciled to Philemon, who was now his brother in Christ, and Paul agreed that it was the right thing to do. They could not control how Philemon would react upon seeing Onesimus, so they would have to act on faith that the gospel would be stronger than one man's transgression against another—a scenario that, for Onesimus and Philemon, ran both ways.

Paul said to Onesimus, "I have been working on a letter to the church that meets in Philemon's home, your old home. I will send you and our brother Tychicus to deliver it, along with another letter from me to him about you."

———

Philemon was a leader in the church in Colossae. When he saw Onesimus standing in his doorway, Philemon had to wrestle internally with what the law permitted and what his faith required. What would he do with the anger he felt in his heart toward Onesimus? With his sense of betrayal? With the fact that Onesimus was now a Christian? Their shared faith changed not only who they were but who they were to each other.

Philemon's life had been transformed by the work of Jesus. Who he'd been before he met Christ was not who he was now. He had become a man with a reputation for love and faith. He poured himself out for the benefit of others, and people's lives were changed by Christ as a result.

Philemon took the personal letter from his runaway and began to read.

"My brother," Paul said in his letter to Philemon, "the same grace you so effectively apply to others has taken hold of Onesimus. As sure as you are a changed man, so is he. Christ has overcome his past just as he overcame yours. Now all that matters between the two of you is what happens next. If Jesus has changed both of you, then I ask you: Who are you to each other? Perhaps this is the reason you and Onesimus were parted for a season—so that you might have him back, no longer as a slave but as a brother."

All three of these men had been transformed by Jesus. Being present for Onesimus's and Philemon's conversions, Paul held a deep affection for them both. He wasn't just contending for Onesimus in this letter; he was pastoring his friend Philemon. God was moving all three of them deeper and deeper into his unfolding purpose for their lives—a purpose to redeem the lost while bringing glory to his Son, who was their peace.

As Philemon read the letter, he remembered Paul's gift for persuasion. "Look," Paul's letter continued. "I could command you to do what I am about to ask, but I don't want to. I want to give you room to respond with your heart. I want you to think, to love, and to live under the banner of the truth that Christ changes us. Your runaway slave has become like my son. And I his imprisoned father. Onesimus gave himself in service to me. For that I am grateful. He has been very useful and I have regarded his service as though it came from you. Your servant Onesimus has become my heart. If there is anything he owes you, name the price. I will repay it. And I will not ask you to repay what you owe me, which is your life. If you consider me your partner in the faith, receive Onesimus as you would receive me."

Philemon smiled at this bit of rhetorical flourish. Paul was saying, in essence, "I gave you the hope of eternal life—and now I have taken Onesimus's debt. How much do I owe you?"

Money aside, Philemon had to do more than forgive a debt. Paul hadn't just sent him the letter about Onesimus—he had sent Onesimus to deliver it. Paul wanted Philemon to receive Onesimus back as a brother. Onesimus wanted this too. The proof was in the fact that, just as his escape had led him twelve hundred miles away, so now his desire to be reconciled brought him twelve hundred miles home.

Paul would have been glad to keep Onesimus, but there was, in fact, a particular opportunity they owed Philemon—the chance for him to receive his slave back as a brother. To forgive Onesimus was to take him as an equal, which not only forgave what was in the past but renewed the purpose for their future together.

Paul appealed to these two participants in the system of slavery to see each other's inherent dignity as a brother in Christ. This was deeply abolitionistic. The gospel of Jesus undermined any hint of any right one person could claim over another as his or her own personal property. Instead it set the example that their lives should be offered up for the sake of each other.

Because of Christ, Philemon and Onesimus were now brothers. This truth lay at the heart of Christianity. There was no longer slave or free, Jew or Gentile, male or female. All were one in Christ Jesus. This was the impact of their new faith, and it was revolutionary.

The faith that took hold of Paul, Philemon, and Onesimus continues to this day, making families out of strangers and friends out of enemies. Though the plan for the church of Jesus Christ dates back to the days before Eden—that mysterious era before time began—its visible formation came together when a man from Nazareth was crucified, died, and was buried and on the third day rose again.

2

ASCENSION

Acts 1:1-26

*J*ESUS OF NAZARETH'S DEATH did not bring an end to his ministry. Rather, his crucifixion at the hands of Pilate and the chief priests fanned into flames a movement that would reach around the world and down through time. The reason? Jesus' death did not end with a corpse on a slab. It ended with resurrection—a real, bodily resurrection and a truly empty tomb.

Three days after Jesus was buried, he rose from the grave and appeared to his disciples. Over the course of the next forty days, the resurrected Jesus, with his nail-pierced hands and spear-split side, spent time in the company of his friends—teaching them, encouraging them, and preparing them for a mission to take the story of his resurrection to the furthest reaches of the globe.

On one of those occasions, as Jesus was eating with his friends, he told them to wait for the gift the Father had promised—the Holy

Spirit Jesus had told them about. The Holy Spirit would come and comfort them and lead them forward. They were to remain in Jerusalem until this happened.

It could not have been easy for the disciples to sit with their risen Lord. For as much joy and hope as Jesus' resurrection brought them, they had been present at his death. They had witnessed the brutal execution of this man they loved, followed, and gave their lives to serving. They saw his beaten and bloody form hang from the cross as he breathed his last. After he died, they were hollowed out with grief.

Along with their grief was the guilt. The trauma of the crucifixion had revealed weaknesses in each one of them. They watched their loyalty to Jesus collapse under the weight of the chief priests' resolve to put an end to what he had started. Not one of them had shown the strength they believed they possessed when Jesus was taken into custody. Each one denied knowing him in his greatest hour of need.

On top of the grief and the guilt was the fact that the world as they knew it had changed. When the resurrected Jesus appeared to his disciples, it was to remind them of their call to be his witnesses in the world. But after the resurrection, they hardly knew what that world was anymore.

They were fragile and unsettled, but they could not escape the reality that Jesus had in fact risen. And they knew they were somehow tied up in it. How could they not be? In a world where everyone dies, one man's resurrection becomes instantly relevant to all. His resurrection was part of their story.

The disciples used that time to ask questions of Jesus. They wanted to understand what would happen next. Would he deal with the religious leaders who opposed him? Would he overthrow Rome? Would he restore the kingdom of Israel to her former glory? And if so, when? Would they be part of it?

Jesus told them the Father was establishing his kingdom, but the particulars of this business were not theirs to know. Such knowledge belonged to God alone. What he could tell them, however, was that the Holy Spirit would come on each one of them in a matter of days, and when he did, they would be filled with power.

In that power, they would be his witnesses in Jerusalem, in Judea and Samaria, and to the ends of the earth. This Great Commission, the disciples came to understand, was very much about the kingdom of God. Their mission, though they struggled to grasp it, was in some way the work of building the kingdom of God. The Holy Spirit and the kingdom of God—the two main subjects Jesus discussed after his resurrection—were inseparably linked, meaning the disciples' call to bear witness to Christ carried eternal significance.

Forty days after the resurrection the disciples were on the Mount of Olives and Jesus was with them. He told them they would be his witnesses, and after he said this, he began to rise up into the sky right before their eyes. Up he went, until a cloud hid him from their sight. The disciples stood in silence as they watched him go. In that moment the world became an even greater mystery than the one the resurrection demanded they embrace.

Jesus did not need to visibly ascend. What the disciples witnessed was not for Jesus' benefit but for theirs. He did it so they would know he was actually gone. They would not see him the next day. He would not attend to them in the same way he had these past forty days. They were not to wait for him. Now they were to wait for the Holy Spirit.

As the disciples stood, looking up and watching their friend vanish, two angelic beings dressed in white appeared. The luminous apparitions said, "Men of Galilee, why are you standing here looking into the sky? This same Jesus who has now been taken up will come again. He will descend in the same way you saw him ascend into heaven. He is coming back."

But as far as the disciples were concerned, the time for standing around and looking up to heaven had passed. They needed to let Jesus go and step into the mission he had given them. What was happening in the sky was not their chief concern. What was happening on earth was.

The disciples responded by obeying Jesus' command to wait. They left the Mount of Olives and went back into Jerusalem and gathered many of Jesus' followers together in the upper room where they were staying.

More than 120 people were gathered in all. There were the eleven disciples: Simon Peter, James and John (the sons of Zebedee), Peter's brother Andrew, Philip, Thomas, Bartholomew, Matthew the tax collector, Simon the zealot, Alphaeus's son James, and James's son Judas. With them were the women who had discovered the empty tomb, Jesus' mother, Mary, Jesus' brothers, and many more whose lives had been changed by Jesus.

For ten days they waited, but it was not a passive waiting. They used the time. They joined together to pray. They prepared for the work that lay ahead. This was an act of obedience to their slain and risen Lord. In their waiting they trusted him, even though their understanding of what lay ahead was less than clear.

Jesus never told them how long they would have to wait for the Holy Spirit to come—just that he would arrive in a little while. After all that had transpired in Jerusalem in recent weeks, remaining there was as much an act of courage as it was an act of faith. This was the city where Jesus had been arrested, beaten, crucified, and buried. This was the place where Judas had betrayed Jesus for a pocket full of silver and where Peter had denied knowing Jesus for fear of a child's accusation. This was the city that seemed bent on erasing any trace of the movement Jesus started.

There were more appealing places to wait and families many of them could have gone home to. Each had the option to return to their homes in places like Galilee, Nazareth, and Cana. They could have gone back to their old jobs—fishing, collecting taxes, carpentry, prostitution. They could have even gone back to their old religions—Judaism or Roman paganism. But those who gathered in the upper room didn't. They chose to obey Christ, and they waited. And they used their time.

Each person gathered in that upper room over the course of those days had been changed in some way through their relationship with Jesus. The cast of characters would have included people like Mary Magdalene, who had once been possessed by demons, and Nicodemus, the Pharisee who helped cover the cost of Jesus' burial. Perhaps the synagogue ruler from Capernaum, Jairus, was there with his daughter Talitha, whom Jesus had raised from the dead, and perhaps they were huddled together in friendship with Lazarus, whom Jesus had also raised from the dead. Former lepers, newly sighted blind people, and once-paralyzed beggars would have been milling about in the crowd too.

As it has always been with the people of God, their desire to obey Christ was strengthened by the bond of their fellowship with one another. God had made them to need one another—to be known, loved, and supported. This was the power and influence of Jesus in each of their lives. He had loved and served them in such a way that they had come to need one another. The usual dividing lines of the day—wealth, nationality, reputation—were already beginning to blur. These were people who had come to accept that they were all weak and that Jesus had been strong for them. They were all poor and Jesus had been generous with them. They were all outsiders and Jesus had given them a place with him. These truths drew them toward one another.

As they waited, they also spent time in devotion to God. They gathered regularly to pray. For what? Certainly for the Holy Spirit to come. But they also asked the Lord to prepare them for the calling he had given them—to bear witness to the true, global, eternal gospel of their resurrected Lord. As they thought about and prayed for the world Jesus meant to change, they considered the changes already begun in them. Many in this group were completely different people than they had been before they met Jesus.

They prayed and they read Scripture. Knowing that the Holy Spirit was coming, they searched the Scriptures to learn what they, as the firstfruits of the budding church on earth, ought to be doing in preparation for the Holy Spirit's coming. In this way, as people have done down through time and around the globe, the disciples spent their time in two-way conversation with God—talking to him through prayer and listening to him through Scripture.

As they prepared for the Holy Spirit's coming, the disciples set out to restore their brotherhood by replacing Judas Iscariot, who had betrayed Jesus and then taken his own life. Scripture told them to do this. Judas' replacement needed to be someone who had been with the disciples for the duration of Jesus's ministry, from John's baptism through to Jesus' ascension. He needed to be someone who had been a witness not only to Jesus' life but also to his death and resurrection. Two men fit these requirements—Justus and Matthias. The eleven disciples left the business of choosing in the hands of God by casting lots to determine who would replace Judas.

The lot fell to Matthias, and he joined their number. And not a moment too soon, because in a matter of only a few days, their band of 120 disciples would grow to a number no one could have imagined. The death of Jesus did not bring his ministry to an end. It fanned it into flames.

PENTECOST

Acts 2:1-47

WHEN THE DAY OF PENTECOST ARRIVED, fifty days after the Passover when Jesus had died, his disciples were all gathered together in Jerusalem. The city was filled with God-fearing pilgrims who had come from every nation, speaking every language.

Pentecost was the feast of the firstfruits of the harvest. Since Israel's early days, God's people had been gathering to bring the first gleanings of their harvest as an offering of thanksgiving and celebration to the Lord. Along with the harvest celebration, Pentecost also commemorated the day the Lord, coming down as a pillar of fire and smoke and power, delivered his law to Moses on Mount Sinai. God-fearers from all around the world returned to Jerusalem to observe the holy day.

It was on this day that the Lord chose to make his presence known again and to sow the firstfruits of the church. On that first

Pentecost after the resurrection, the Holy Spirit came down like a mighty rush of wind and descended like tongues of fire on each of the disciples gathered there. They began to speak in other languages as the Holy Spirit enabled them. When this happened, sojourners from Libya, Parthia, Mesopotamia, Asia, Egypt, Rome, and all points in between came together in wonder because they were hearing the followers of Jesus proclaim the wonders of God, each in their own native tongue.

What had separated the nations since the days of Babel—the confusion of multiple languages—was coming undone. A single message was suddenly being understood by all. When the disciples of Jesus saw the tongues of fire come to rest on one another, the image was clear—the Holy Spirit was equipping them to do what Christ had commissioned them to do: testify. The Holy Spirit was becoming the voice through which they would proclaim the gospel to otherwise spiritually dead souls.

The arrival of the Holy Spirit at Pentecost was the undoing of Babel. At Babel the people of God had all been together in one place, all speaking a common language and trying to build a tower to the heavens to prove they were mighty enough to come to where God was. Here at Pentecost, God-fearing people from every nation were gathered, separated by their many languages, and the Holy Spirit of God was coming down to them and restoring their ability to hear one another bear witness to the wonders of God. That had not been the case since the workers on the tower of Babel set down their tools and walked away, confused by their sudden inability to understand one another.

Many people gathered there in Jerusalem on that Pentecost saw the Holy Spirit descend on Jesus' disciples. They heard the message of salvation in their own language, and though there were some cynics in the crowd who said the disciples were drunk, many were amazed at what they saw and wondered what it all meant.

Simon Peter stepped forward, the other eleven disciples with him, and he called for the crowd to listen. Simon Peter, who only weeks earlier had denied knowing Jesus, was now filled and empowered by the Holy Spirit. He began to speak.

Peter said, "Listen to me, you who live here in Jerusalem and wonder what has just happened. I will explain it to you. No one here is drunk. It is only nine in the morning. No, what you're seeing has been spoken of by the prophets of old."

Quoting the scriptures, Peter reminded them that the prophet Joel had foretold the day when God would pour out his Holy Spirit on his people and they would proclaim his mighty wonders. They would perform signs and wonders and call the people to repentance, and all who called on the name of the Lord would be saved. This was that day—a day to call on the name of the Lord and find salvation.

Then Peter told the crowd they should have remembered that God had said his Christ would be known by his resurrection. God had raised Jesus, who was betrayed into the hands of wicked men and nailed to a cross, and freed him from the agony of death. Death could not hold him. David had written a psalm about this, saying that God's holy one would not see decay in the grave. David was not writing about himself, Peter said. His grave was nearby, and his remains were in it. They could see this for themselves. No, David was speaking about the Messiah, who would live after dying and who would establish the path of life that would lead to eternal joy in the presence of God.

Peter then brought his message home by quoting another psalm from David, which spoke of the place God's holy one would occupy. The Messiah would be seated at the right hand of God and reign as King—a king from David's line, the King of all kings.

Peter said, "This King is Jesus, whom God has raised to life. His body has not seen decay, and you are witnesses to this fact. You've seen it yourselves. Jesus has been exalted to the right hand of God, and today he has given the Father's promised gift of the Holy Spirit. So listen and believe what I'm saying: God has made Jesus, whom you crucified, both Lord and Christ."

Peter's sermon did not aim to establish a new religion. Though the Holy Spirit's coming at Pentecost marked the beginning of something new, it was a moment rooted in something ancient—faith in the covenant God of Abraham, Moses, and David. Peter's sermon addressed a longing people have had since the foundation of the world—the ability to call on the name of their Maker and be safe.

The people listening to Peter were cut to the heart. They were convicted of their sin and need for Christ. So they said to Peter and the other eleven apostles, "Is there hope for us? What do we need to do in order to be saved?"

Peter said, "This message is for you. It is for you and for the generations everywhere to come—for all whom the Lord will call to himself. Repent and be baptized in the name of Jesus for the forgiveness of your sins."

Peter went on, speaking many more words under the power of the Holy Spirit; he and the other apostles pleaded with the crowd to put their faith in Jesus as the Messiah, the Savior of sinners. The people responded in ways no one could have imagined. That day more than three thousand people put their faith in Jesus and were baptized in his name.

The days that followed were strange. The apostles continued to minister to their city with boldness, and the Holy Spirit worked through them, performing signs and wonders through the apostles' hands. Those signs and wonders served to validate the apostles' authority to lead the early church. The people were not pooling together their varied spiritual preferences for this new church. Rather they were giving their attention to those who had been set apart by God as the trusted witnesses to the life and ministry of Jesus. This large and growing church devoted themselves to the apostles' teachings and the study of God's Word. They met together regularly to share meals and pray. They shared everything they had with one another. If someone had a need and someone else could meet that need, they did. They lived believing that their lives did not consist in the abundance of their possessions. They embraced the idea that following Jesus meant they lived to serve, not to be served.

Growing in this kind of fellowship meant those with plenty needed to step forward in generosity and those in need had to step forward to receive help—and both needed to be humble about it. This wasn't always easy, but this was the way of Christian fellowship—living as though they belonged to each other, bound together by Christ.

Because they were bound to one another through their shared faith, they did not gather for fellowship alone. They also gathered for worship. They went to the temple courts together; they gathered around the Lord's Table and broke bread together, and they prayed together with glad hearts. Their fellowship and worship was a mix of deep devotion and hearty laughter—reverence without pretense.

The new and growing church loved God and they loved each other. As a result, in those early days anyhow, people looked on these new followers of Jesus with favor, and every day God called more people to place their faith in Christ and be counted among the new fellowship of believers.

The early church bore the marks of study, fellowship, worship, and outreach. This was what it looked like to bear witness to Christ.

It was a fellowship of imperfect people at the beginning of a new era, and one of the characteristics that marked them was their desire to be together and to gather around the Word and table of the Lord.

As this was happening, Peter and the other apostles were growing in their roles as leaders in and around Jerusalem.

4

FLEE TO GOD

Acts 3:1-26

ONE AFTERNOON, NOT LONG AFTER PENTECOST, Peter and John went together to the temple to pray. They passed through the bronze-plated gate called Beautiful, the crown jewel of Jerusalem's gates. By the entrance sat a man who had been paralyzed since birth. The city gate was a strategic place for him to sit because there he could garner the pity of those making their way to the temple for worship—people whose hearts and minds were already set on charity.

This beggar was a fixture in that part of town. People passed by him several times a day as they went in and out of the city. The gate called Beautiful was his post. There he was something of a celebrity, known for his poverty and need. Everyone knew who he was.

When Peter and John passed by the beggar, he asked them for some money. Peter and John stopped and looked at the man. The beggar was not accustomed to people wanting to look him in the eye. Often people tried to pass by as quickly as possible, maybe dropping a coin in his cup as they went. But Peter and John stopped, and Peter said to the man, "Look at us."

The man looked up, expecting to get something from the two men. But Peter said, "I do not have any silver or gold for you."

Most of the crippled man's relational connections by that gate were transactions—him asking for money and people either giving to him or ignoring him. But they did not often stop to talk. These two men standing in front of him wanted to talk. They did not have money but they still had something to give him.

Peter continued, "What I do have, I give to you now. In the name of Jesus Christ of Nazareth, I say to you, stand up and walk."

Peter reached out, took the beggar's right hand, and helped him to his feet. The man could hardly believe what was happening. He had never stood up before, but all of a sudden a strange and powerful sensation ran through his ankles and feet as his atrophied muscles took shape and his tendons and joints aligned. Within a matter of seconds his withered legs became strong enough that he jumped to his feet and began to leap for joy, praising God. The crowd that had gathered marveled at what they saw.

Word of the miracle spread quickly up and down Solomon's Colonnade, and people began to run to the scene to see with their own eyes the wonder they had heard. They arrived to see the newly restored man holding on to Peter and John as he danced and sang.

This was no trick. Those who witnessed the miracle knew this man and his story. What had just happened defied explanation. They did not know why this beggar, crippled since birth, was suddenly able to leap and dance. But there was no disputing the fact that he could. In the space of a day the man shed his poverty and doubled his celebrity.

When Peter saw that the crowd was struck with a mix of astonishment and fear, he raised his hand to get their attention and said,
"Men of Israel, why are you surprised at what you see? Do you think
we made this man walk? Do you think that it was by my power or
John's godliness that this man was able to stand and leap and dance?"
The crowd didn't only want to know; they needed to know how
this man had received his miracle. Though they did not share his
physical malady, each one of them had something in their own lives
they wanted restored. They were a captive audience, planted there by
their own curiosity until Peter explained what they had just witnessed.

Peter said, "Let me tell you what has happened here. I did not heal
this man. No, the God of Abraham, Isaac, and Jacob, the God of your
fathers, glorified his holy one, his Son, Jesus Christ, whom you crucified. You handed this Jesus over to Pontius Pilate to be killed. You
disowned him when Pilate was ready to let him go. You asked Pilate
to release a murderer instead when given the option. Listen to me:
you disowned the holy one of God and killed the author of life. But
God raised him from the dead, and you were witnesses to that too."

Many present in the crowd had been there six weeks earlier when
Jesus was paraded through those very streets, beaten and bloody.
Many of them had cried out for his crucifixion. And now, when all
they wanted to know was how the crippled beggar had become able
to walk, Peter delivered a sermon focused on their complicity in
Jesus' death. What did one have to do with the other? What did the
beggar's healing have to do with Israel's disowning Jesus?

Peter let the question hang in the air before tying the two together.

He said, "It was by faith in the name of Jesus that this man you
see and know was made strong. By the name of Jesus, and through
the faith that comes from him, this man has been healed. And you
are all now witnesses to that as well."

It had never occurred to many in the crowd that they were guilty of disowning the Messiah. Many had spent their whole lives anticipating his coming. But they forgot why he was coming. They had not understood what John the Baptist meant when he said Jesus was the Lamb of God who takes away the sins of the world. In that statement John summarized not only what Jesus had come to do but also how he planned to do it. He had come to take away their sin and to do so by dying as a sacrifice before God on their behalf. This was what the people missed. They expected the Messiah to come more as a lion than a lamb—as someone who would cleanse their land from the pagan Gentiles who had defiled it with their idols and temples. They assumed the Messiah would come and deal with the sins of those around them but not theirs. When they demanded the death of Jesus, they did not understand they were demanding the death of the Messiah.

Peter studied the crowd as his rebuke began to sink in. Many faces had gone from joyful astonishment to silently looking at the ground. Some peeled off from the crowd, unwilling to listen to any more of Peter's indictment. But others stayed and listened. Peter carried no official authority with this crowd, but the truth of his words found its way into their hearts as some began to feel, for the first time, the weight of their guilt.

Peter felt it too. Twice in his speech he told them they had disowned Jesus. As for Peter, he had done it three times.

Peter said, "Some of you acted in ignorance. You did not know what you were doing. The same is true for many of your leaders. They didn't know either. But through Jesus' death, God has fulfilled what the prophets of old predicted—that the Christ would suffer. He would be beaten for our transgressions and crushed for our iniquity. The chastisement that would bring us peace would be laid upon him. God himself would put upon him the iniquity of us all. So flee to God. Repent and return to the one you have sinned against. Flee to him."

The image of fleeing to God was a reference to Israel's ancient cities of refuge. According to the law of Moses, an Israelite could seek asylum in a designated city of refuge if he were guilty of an accidental death. That city would protect him from prosecution and shelter him from his guilt.

Peter told the crowd they had caused an accidental death. They had not known what they were doing, but they were nonetheless complicit in the death of Jesus. They needed refuge from their guilt, and the only refuge available to them was the mercy and forgiveness of the God they had sinned against.

The beauty of running to God for refuge, Peter said, was that when they did, their sins would be wiped away. Their guilt would no longer be counted against them. If they sought mercy at the feet of Christ, they would find it. Their sins would be forgiven, and they would be restored to God.

Peter said, "Pray for Christ to return to restore not only this beggar but every broken thing. He will come again, and when he does it will be to restore all things unto himself. This will happen at the appointed time, but remember that all the prophets from Moses and Samuel on looked forward to that day. Understand this, men of Israel. You are the heirs of those prophets and of the covenant God cut with Abraham. You are the offspring God promised to bless through Abraham's seed. God sent his Messiah to you first. So turn from your sin and flee to God."

People who came to see the lame man who had been healed did not expect to be told that they were guilty of the death of the Messiah. But Peter ended his message with a profound invitation for them to put their faith in Christ. God had not just sent his Messiah into the world. He had sent him to them. They were known. In all their guilt—intended and unintended—they were known and invited to find refuge in the grace of God, accomplished through the life, death, and resurrection of his Son.

And the church continued to grow.

5

PRAYER FOR BOLDNESS

Acts 4:1-31

*T*HE CHURCH GREW AS THE WORDS of the disciples found purchase in the hearts of many who were hearing the gospel of Jesus Christ for the first time and turning to him for their salvation. Another two thousand people came to Christ as the result of Peter's call to repent at Solomon's Colonnade.

But not everyone responded this way.

The leaders of the temple area—the Pharisees, Sadducees, and the temple guard—took offense at Peter and John because they were teaching that Jesus Christ had risen from the dead and saying the religious leaders had crucified God's Messiah. So the captain of the temple guard arrested Peter and John and held them overnight.

In the morning the Sanhedrin, which consisted of the rulers, elders, and scribes, gathered in Jerusalem with Annas, the high priest, and Caiaphas, the chief priest who had plotted Jesus' death and tried him in front of the Sanhedrin before handing him over to Pilate. The issue that lay at the heart of the confrontation was authority. Who had given Peter and John permission to preach as they did in their temple? "By what power and in what name do you do these things?" the teachers of the law demanded of these uneducated men standing in their court.

Peter chose not to give a diplomatic response to the charges against him. Though he could have simply said, "Jesus of Nazareth," he did not. He remembered what Jesus had said concerning the persecution the disciples would face if they followed him. Jesus had told them they would be handed over to local authorities and pressed to give answers for their conduct. He'd said, "When they deliver you over, do not be anxious about what you are to say. It will not be you who will speak, but the Holy Spirit from God speaking through you."

Though at the time Peter wasn't completely certain what Jesus meant when he spoke of the Holy Spirit, ever since Pentecost he'd had a bit more clarity. Peter recognized that he was being given an opportunity he may never have again—a chance to proclaim the gospel to the religious leaders of the day. And he had something to say.

Filled with the Holy Spirit, Peter stepped forward and said, "Are we on trial here for the good deed we did for the crippled man at the Beautiful gate? Are you concerned about where we obtained our power? We do these things by the power and the name of Jesus Christ of Nazareth—whom you crucified and whom God has raised from the dead. May it be known to you and to all Israel that Jesus, the stone you rejected, is in fact the cornerstone upon which all salvation and hope rests."

The boldness of Peter's answer lay in his assumption that Jesus' authority was more than sufficient for him and John to not only work miracles in the temple area but also teach about Jesus.

Peter's response frustrated the temple leaders who had been part of Jesus' crucifixion. But Peter wasn't finished. Not only had they performed that miracle in the name of Jesus, he continued, but that was the only name in which salvation could be found. There in that room filled with religious leaders, adorned in their vestments and surrounded by the elaborate temple architecture—all of which communicated a message of salvation through law-keeping—Peter proclaimed that salvation came through Jesus alone.

The religious leaders were insulted at the notion that they were the ones getting it wrong. But with the formerly crippled man standing beside Peter and John on two perfectly sound legs, the Sanhedrin could think of no reply.

The temple rulers sent Peter and John out of the room so they could confer. Behind closed doors, they speculated about their options. "There is no denying that a miracle has taken place," they said. "Everyone in Jerusalem knows about it by now. The best we can do is try to contain the influence of these disciples of Jesus of Nazareth."

The Sanhedrin summoned Peter and John again and said, "We are going to let you go, but do not teach or speak to anyone any longer in this name."

Peter and John said, "What are we supposed to do? If you need to arrest us, arrest us, but how can we accept your instruction to remain silent when Jesus commands us to testify about him? Whether it is right for us, in the sight of God, to listen to you rather than to him, you must judge. And we will accept your judgment and its consequences. But we cannot and will not remain silent."

There was a tenor of respect in Peter's objection. He acknowledged these leaders' civil authority. He was not flagrantly dismissing the role of temple court. He was acknowledging that the authority of Jesus was higher than the laws of the land, and when the two were in conflict, civil law could not bind his conscience against the law of his God. Peter and John were men under authority. Their lives were not their own. The name they were being told to disavow was the name by which they lived. How could they do what the temple court was asking?

The temple court knew punishing Peter and John would be extremely unpopular, since it seemed the whole city was praising God on account of the miracle they had performed. So they threatened Peter and John with the consequences of what would happen if they continued and then let them go.

This threat from the temple leaders was not empty. It carried a reminder of what they'd done to Jesus himself. So when the disciples were warned and sent away, they went to their friends and told them what the chief priests and elders had said. Peter and John brought the burden of their persecution and hardship to the church. This was not their burden to carry alone. It was a threat against the church itself.

Immediately the church gathered together and sought the Lord in prayer. Scripture had taught them that persecution was nothing new to God, so they prayed, "Sovereign Lord, who made the heavens and the earth and the sea and all that is in them, hear us. Through the mouth of your servant David, the Holy Spirit said, 'Why do the nations plot against the Lord God Almighty? They plot in vain. They cannot oppose you, though they still try.' In this city people have gathered together against your holy servant Jesus, whom you anointed. Though Herod and Pilate, along with the Gentiles and the people of Israel, have opposed Jesus, they are nevertheless participating in what you have determined should take place. The death of your own son did not happen apart from your will. If you were sovereign over that, then surely you are sovereign over this threat of persecution that has now come to us. Please, Lord, look on your servants and give us boldness to continue to speak, lest we wither away in fear. Continue to perform signs and wonders through our hands, and give us the courage to continue speaking and teaching in your name. Stretch out your hand to heal. Work through us in the name of your holy servant Jesus."

All through Peter and John's hearing before the Sanhedrin, not once did they try to plead for mercy. In fact, Peter did the opposite of what a man who was trying to escape trouble would do. When the leaders of the temple warned him to no longer speak in Jesus' name, Peter boldly and flatly told them no. They could not obey this command.

For these early believers, Christ was the light by which they saw the world. Nothing made any sense apart from him. In the face of persecution, they prayed for Christ's name to be glorified—for his light to shine brighter. They were contending for Jesus' name, not for their own reputations, because they understood that the simmering opposition they faced was not ultimately against them but against the Lord. So when they prayed, they did not ask for safety but for courage. They prayed against fear and the listlessness that can so easily overtake people who feel threatened. They prayed that their passion would be stronger for his glory than for their comfort.

They prayed that the Lord would continue to stretch out his hand to heal and that signs and wonders would continue to be performed in the name of Jesus—which is precisely what stirred up all the trouble in the first place. They asked the Lord to continue pouring out his redemptive healing and grace on their broken world.

As they were praying for boldness, the place where they had gathered began to quake. It started as a subtle tremor, but soon the entire room shook. The people understood this as an answer to their prayer. God himself was shaking their gathering. He heard them. He wasn't sleeping or distant or unconcerned. By shaking that room, God reminded them that he was the maker and ruler of all and that he was with them.

After that day, the disciples, filled with the Holy Spirit, continued to preach the resurrection of Jesus Christ, and God gave them what they asked for—boldness.

6

ANANIAS AND SAPPHIRA

Acts 4:32–5:11

THE APOSTLES—PETER, JOHN, and the others—continued to preach the resurrection of Jesus Christ, and they did so with great power. Peace was on them as they continued their work, though the rulers of the temple did not share that same spirit.

Difficulty has a way of bringing people together. After the Sanhedrin threatened the disciples and told them to no longer speak in Jesus' name, the new church grew even more in unity and affection for one another.

These new Christians were united in heart and soul. They were of one mind. They carried each other's burdens. They were brave for one another, encouraging their brothers and sisters when they became afraid and reminding each other of the reason they were bound together.

They were becoming for one another a model of what Jesus had prayed they would be. On the night he was betrayed, as he was gathered in an upper room with his disciples, Jesus prayed for their unity. He asked God to make his disciples one, just as he and the Father were one. He prayed that they would be so joined in heart and mind that the world would look at their love for one another and, as a result, believe that Jesus was sent from God.

Jesus wanted the same glory that rested on him to rest on them so they would be one. He prayed, "May I be in them just as you are in me, so that the world will know that you have loved them and sent me as proof of your love."

The unity these early Christians sought was forged in the furnace of diversity. When they first came together at Pentecost, they were a group of people from all over the world—Egypt, Asia, Rome, Mesopotamia, Libya, Cyrene, and Judea. They came from many places with all sorts of cultural customs, languages, and dress.

Since the days of the first sons of Adam, people have resented and opposed those who were different from themselves—even to the point of murder. Yet here in the face of persecution that threatened death, people from all over the world were joining together in a unity marked by more than words. They were bound to each other by Christ. Theirs was a unity not of sameness but of purpose—proclaiming the resurrection of Jesus.

They were united in faith, but their unity didn't end there. They were also united in their material possessions. These Christians didn't just share the bonds of friendship. They shared everything they owned. Many of the thousands who put their faith in Jesus were poor—either by lack of resources or distance from them. So followers of Jesus began to sell their possessions—land, houses, and other items of value—and they laid the proceeds of their sales at the apostles' feet so that no one among them would have to be in need.

They were marked by a posture of generosity. They regarded their wealth as a river that ran through their lives. Resources would come and go. In some seasons the river would be a rushing torrent; in others it was a trickle. But the highest value or purpose they could assign to the river of wealth that ran through their hands was the care of those in need. God tightened their hold on each other as he loosened their grip on their possessions.

One of the men who modeled this spirit of generosity was named Barnabas. He was a Levite and a native of Cyprus. Barnabas was an encourager. He was a source of strength for the people around him. He believed in God's goodness and power in the face of their dangerous circumstances. While the early church was figuring out how to care for their own, and as people pooled their resources to help meet the needs of the poor, Barnabas sold a plot of land he owned and gave the proceeds to the apostles, who used the money to care for the needy. Barnabas's gift was not compulsory but voluntary—a proportional response to the needs he saw around him.

Barnabas reasoned that if God did not spare his own son but gave him up for them all, how would he not also with Jesus graciously give his people everything they needed for all that they were called to do and be? If everything Barnabas needed came from God, and these were the people with whom he shared the work of the gospel, then how could he not also generously share what he had too?

Barnabas and the other Christians were united in faith and in their possessions because they were united in a common work— boldly proclaiming Christ. This was the work that joined them together. When they prayed for courage, it was not only so they might keep preaching but also so they might keep trusting in Christ

for all things. This generous spirit toward one another came to
define the early Christians in the eyes of the world. People watched
the way the lived and came to say, "See how these Christian people
love one another!"

Another man in the church named Ananias owned a field. He
and his wife discussed the idea of selling the land and giving the
proceeds to the apostles, as Barnabas and others had done. They
decided to withhold a portion of the sale price for themselves,
which they were free to do. But Ananias and his wife, Sapphira, did
not want to appear stingy, so they agreed that they would tell the
apostles that the amount they gave was everything they had gained
from the sale.

Their willingness to help their new brothers and sisters in need
was noble, but their hearts were conflicted. Though they were
willing to give, and give generously, they also wanted to appear
selfless in their generosity without having to actually be selfless.
They chose the path of deception to make themselves look like
better people.

Ananias brought a large sum to Peter and John and the other
apostles, and he led them to believe he was giving them everything
he had gained from the sale. Peter, filled with the Holy Spirit, sensed
that something was off.

Peter asked Ananias, "Is this the full amount of the sale?"

Nervous but committed to his course, Ananias nodded.

Peter said, "Ananias, why are you lying? What are you trying to
gain here by misrepresenting your generosity? Satan has filled your
heart to lie to the Holy Spirit. That whole time the land was yours,
was it not yours to do with as you pleased? And after you sold it,
were not the proceeds yours to do with as you saw fit? You were free
to give as little or as much as you wanted. But you wanted to look

more generous than you really are. And you wanted glory for that. Your deception was not against men. It was against God."

When Peter said this, Ananias felt a great pressure in his chest. He fell over and died.

When the apostles and all who were gathered saw Ananias die, they were overcome with fear. Stunned, confused, and afraid, everyone stood silently, taking in what had just happened. A couple of the young men went to Ananias's body, wrapped him up, and carried him out to bury him. As word about what had happened to Ananias spread among the disciples, so did their fear.

After about three hours, Ananias's wife, Sapphira, returned and came in to where the apostles had gathered. She did not yet know what had happened to her husband.

When Peter saw her, he said, "Tell me, Sapphira. For how much did you sell your field?"

Those who had been there when Ananias died leaned forward, pleading in their hearts for her to speak the truth. But Sapphira gave Peter and the others the same number her husband had reported.

Peter said, "Why did you and your husband agree together to put the Spirit of God to the test?"

A look of fear spread across her face as she saw the somber expressions of the others in the room.

Peter continued, "The feet of those who buried your husband are here to carry you out as well."

Like her husband, Sapphira fell down and died. The young men who had buried her husband took her out and laid her to rest beside him. Great fear gripped the community. What were they to make of such a tragedy? There was not a person among them who had not at some point tried to make themselves appear better than they actually were. Would such a fate find them too? What sort of God was this?

He was not a God who demanded that they give away their possessions. People were free to give what they had decided in their hearts to give. They were meant to be a people who thought through what their contributions to the church should be. The apostles didn't decide this for them.

How people handle their finances often gives a truer picture than words alone of where their hearts are when it comes to their trust and fear of God. Projecting a generosity that is less than what is true is a quest for personal glory apart from God. Such a quest springs from an absence of a genuine fear of a Holy God.

Ananias and Sapphira died as the result of their sin. All who heard of it were filled with fear. If God was Holy, if God was all-powerful, if God's demand for righteousness could be satisfied only by the sacrifice of his son, Jesus Christ, on their behalf, then they were right to fear him. It is always a kind of grace when God calls his people to fear him. He is the author of life and its span, and to regard him as anything less is to live as though he is not real.

Still, the tragedy of Ananias and Sapphira brought with it a sobering sense of reverence. The people who had just asked the Lord for the courage to stand true in the face of outside persecution suddenly felt a fear to examine what dwelled within themselves.

7

GAMALIEL'S WAGER

Acts 5:12-42

J ERUSALEM WAS CHANGING. Ever since the Passover when Jesus
was killed and three days later rose from the grave, people in and
around the city had begun to develop a new sort of spiritual curiosity. Great things had happened in that region—miracles that
stoked in the hearts of many a sense of wonder that hadn't been felt
there since the days of King David.

The significance of Solomon's Portico grew for the followers of
Christ. It took courage for people to stand there and identify themselves as followers of Christ. People had to decide just how public
they were willing to be about their faith. They had to weigh how
much of their lives it would occupy. For some, this proved too
costly. For a growing number, however, Solomon's Portico was becoming a sacred space. Like a place that called to mind a memory
or a face or a sober sense of meaning, that hall put a lump in the

throat of many who had seen their lives change when they encountered Jesus there.

Some new Christians stayed away out of fear. There were plenty of reasons a reasonable person would want to keep their distance from the apostles at Solomon's Portico. To begin with, it was near here where their leader and founder, Jesus, had been publicly beaten, mocked, and crucified not more than a few months earlier. People in Jerusalem remembered how this spectacle was carried out with great zeal both by the religious community and the Roman authorities. No one in power in Jerusalem, it seemed then, had wanted Jesus alive.

Second, there was the current outside pressure to stay away. The people who had put Jesus to death told Peter and John to no longer speak in his name. With this warning came the understood threat: "What we did to him we can do to you as well. Don't test us."

Third, after the deaths of Ananias and Sapphira, many professing Christians felt pressure from within their own fellowship to consider just how devoted they were. Their new religion was beginning to appear very unsafe.

But the believers continued to meet at Solomon's Portico, and the church continued to grow. For the apostles this was no time to be afraid—it was a time for action. Peter and John and the other apostles returned to that place every day, preaching and healing, and more people than ever put their faith in Jesus—men and women alike.

People brought their afflicted loved ones to Peter, and they were healed. People from the outlying regions soon began to flock to the Portico as well, laying their loved ones on mats in the streets, hoping that Peter might pass by and that his shadow might fall on them so they would be healed. And they were.

The apostles continued to meet at Solomon's Portico because they were driven by something stronger than fear. They remembered how Jesus had spoken of the people's need for reconciliation with God and how he alone could accomplish that reconciliation. Many people had turned away from him when he talked like this. On one occasion, after many deserted Jesus, unable to embrace his teaching, he asked his disciples, "Will you leave too?"

Peter had said, "To whom shall we go, Lord? You alone have the words of life."

Now filled with the Holy Spirit, Peter understood and believed his own confession more than ever. He and the other apostles believed Jesus had come to give them something they desperately needed—reconciliation with God.

The apostles continued to preach and heal and they were held in high esteem. They had a credible witness because they lived out their faith regardless of the price. There was a cost to being genuine, and people knew it. The apostles' boldness to continue seeking the Lord in the face of opposition demonstrated to the world that they believed what they confessed. Every facet of their lives was invested in their faith in Christ.

People from neighboring communities began to come to them and put their faith in Jesus as well. The gospel was beginning to move from its epicenter in Jerusalem, finding influence in the outlying regions of Judea and Samaria.

The high priest boiled with jealousy over the way people were so taken with Peter and the other apostles. He was angry at their boldness to return to this place to preach. The temple leadership had meant what they said about staying away, so they arrested the apostles and put them in a public prison.

That night an angel of the Lord appeared to the apostles in the prison and opened the cell doors. The angel told them to return to the temple—where they'd been arrested—and continue teaching the things for which they were arrested. As morning broke, the apostle did just that. They went into the temple area and began to preach about the life that comes only through faith in Jesus.

That morning the temple council assembled and sent for the apostles to be brought from the prison to stand trial. But the guards discovered that though the cells were locked and undisturbed, the apostles were not in them. They had escaped. The guards' first thought was that they had slipped away into hiding. But it did not take long for the search party to find them back in the temple, once again preaching to a captive audience.

It was embarrassing for the authorities to have to arrest the apostles again. Plus there was the possible public relations nightmare of the temple leaders looking like bullies—they were harassing men who, as far as most people could tell, were only having a positive impact on the society, bringing healing to the sick and hope to the hopeless.

But the religious leaders were committed to their process, so they arrested the apostles a third time—only gently, so as not to arouse the ire of the people who were quickly growing to respect and love these followers of Jesus Christ. They arrested them again, and the apostles went peacefully. The guards marched them before the temple council, where the council members asked why they continued to preach in Jesus' name.

Peter answered for the group: "We must obey God rather than men. The God of our fathers raised Jesus, whom you crucified. And God has exalted him to his right hand as the ruler and leader of his people in order to call us to repentance and grant us forgiveness.

We are witnesses to this, and so is the Holy Spirit, whom God has given to all who obey him."

This message outlining Jesus' crucifixion, resurrection, and ascension, and the apostles' role as eyewitnesses, would become Peter's standard response when he was asked to defend why he spoke in Jesus' name. The sermon structure confronted the hearer with their guilt while offering the assurance of hope. But those who were seeking to shut down the apostles' voice resented the notion that they were in the wrong.

Peter's boldness enraged the council. But it was more complicated than that. Back when they had first arrested the apostles, they had made the dubious observation that Jesus' followers were uneducated men. And yet somehow these men—who had come nowhere close to logging the hours of study the council members had—were suddenly vastly more popular in people's eyes. And the apostles didn't seem to fear the council or consider themselves subject to their authority.

As the religious leaders' anger flared, they considered killing the disciples right then and there as Peter spoke. But an unlikely arbiter spoke up—Gamaliel. Gamaliel was a teacher of the law. He was well-respected and deeply influential among the Pharisees in his day. He was a leader whose words carried great weight. He was a wise and observant man, and he saw that his council was about to do something based on an emotional response that might end up costing them in the long run.

Gamaliel noticed that there were significant disconnects between the actions of the apostles and the reactions of the council—variances that allowed at least the shadow of a possibility that there was something to the witness of the apostles. First, the temple council had authority on their side, yet they were acting as though they needed to reclaim their authority over the Christians. Second, the popularity of these apostles was built around miracles they performed in the name of Jesus—miracles that were both undeniable and beneficial for the community. Third, throughout all the persecution the Christians had faced, they had remained astonishingly focused on their message. After they were arrested and commanded not to speak in Jesus' name any longer, this was the very thing they continued to do—and very much out in the open. Their message wasn't political. They weren't calling for social reform. They weren't attempting to introduce a new god to worship. If they were driven by greed or a lust for power, surely they would have chosen a more effective place to rally their followers into action than the temple where they kept getting arrested. But they didn't. They stayed in the same place in the face of persecution—undeterred from the gospel.

These facts didn't add up for Gamaliel. He said to the council, "You know that when leaders of movements are killed, men like Theudas or Judas the Galilean, their followers tend to give up. If Jesus was a man like one of these, what these men are doing will soon fall apart. But if this is of God we cannot stop it, and we may actually find ourselves opposing God in the process. We should consider this."

Gamaliel had seen enough to know that things were not always as they seemed. So he wagered that there was at least a shred of possibility that the Christians were speaking truth, and if they were, no one would be able to silence them. Gamaliel was willing to wait and see if the apostles were in fact on to something he had missed up to this point. To raise this point was to acknowledge that he might have to change his mind. They all might. But he persuaded them that his was the way of wisdom.

When the council agreed to Gamaliel's advice, they beat the apostles, threatened them again, and released them. Again. The apostles rejoiced that they had been counted worthy to suffer dishonor for Christ's sake. They went right back to teaching in the temple and also began going house to house, preaching in Jesus' name.

8

STEPHEN AND SAUL

Acts 6:1–8:1

*A*s the church continued to grow in Jerusalem, some of the believers raised a complaint with the apostles. The church was largely made up of Hebrews—Jews who lived in Israel and spoke Aramaic, and Hellenists—Jews who had remained in the countries they had been carried off to during the exiles and spoke Greek.

The temple authorities in Jerusalem provided a measure of care and assistance to Hebrew widows, but the Hellenist widows were not given the same care. Many of the Hellenist Christians went to the apostles to complain that their widows were not being cared for in the same way the Hebrew widows were.

The church was continuing to grow by the hundreds, and many of their number needed care they could not find through the ordinary civil channels. The church had already taken the position that they would share what they had in common so no one would be in need. This meant that in their community there could be no Hebrew widows and Hellenistic widows—only Christian widows. So the apostles gathered the entire community and said, "We cannot personally tend to all of the particular needs within our fellowship. It would not be right for the twelve of us to set aside our ministry of the Word of God to tend to every need that arises."

They decided they would choose deacons from their number—godly men with wisdom and good reputations who would focus on caring for the dignity of the lonely and aged image-bearers of God who lived among them. They chose seven men: Stephen, Philip, Prochorus, Nicanor, Timon, Parmenus, and Nicolaus. These were men with Greek names—Hellenists. The apostles laid hands on these deacons and set them apart for the work of care.

The apostles continued to preach and teach. The Word of God continued to go out, and the number of disciples in Jerusalem increased greatly. In fact, many of the priests were beginning to put their faith in Christ. Gamaliel's wisdom was proving to be true—the Christians were not going away anytime soon.

As soon as the deacons were selected, they got to work. Stephen, who was full of the Holy Spirit, had been performing miracles among the people, healing the sick. A group of men from the synagogue gathered to try to expose Stephen as a fraud, but when they questioned him, he spoke with a wisdom and power they could not refute or minimize. This only frustrated them further, so they colluded with some of the men in the temple area and had them bring charges of heresy against Stephen, claiming they heard him say blasphemous things against Moses and even God himself.

Hearing this, the crowd turned against Stephen. The temple elders grabbed him and brought him to stand trial before the temple authorities. Several false witnesses came and spoke against Stephen, saying he was constantly defaming the temple and the Scriptures. As Stephen stood under the weight of these accusations, several people noticed that his face bore the calm of an angel. He was unafraid.

The high priest, who had overseen the prosecution of Jesus, asked Stephen to give his defense against the charges being leveled against him.

Stephen said, "Brothers and fathers, listen to me." He proceeded to walk the court through their own history. Retracing the stories of Abraham, Isaac, Joseph, Moses, Joshua, David, Solomon, and the prophets, Stephen spoke of how the people of God, down through time, had rebelled against God at every turn—making idols of gold and land and law-keeping. The land, the temple, and the law had become for the people of Israel their basis for God's favor. They believed that as long as they occupied the land, kept the law of Moses, and maintained their temple practices, God would keep them as his own. They embraced these as their hope of salvation.

Stephen said the people believed that as long as they possessed the land of Israel, they possessed God's blessing—as though God's affection for them was tied to real estate. They lived as though God's intent was to lead them to this place and cloister them off from the rest of the world—lavishing them alone with blessing. They had forgotten that God's design for the sons of Abraham was that all the nations of the earth would be blessed through them.

Stephen told the temple authorities that it was a misuse of the law of Moses for them to look to it for their redemption. God gave the law in part to show that they couldn't meet God's righteous requirements on their own. The law was given so they might look for the Messiah to come and be their redeemer, having found the law to be an impossible standard. But instead of rising to the righteousness God required, the people merely lowered the standard, reducing the law to lists of rules and regulations without regard for the condition of the heart. Stephen, who stood accused of rejecting the law, told the religious leaders they had been rejecting the law of Moses their whole lives because they were now rejecting Christ.

"You are stiff-necked and uncircumcised in your hearts and ears," Stephen said. "As your fathers before you have always done, you too now reject the Holy Spirit. Name a prophet you didn't persecute. Name one you didn't kill when they announced your need for the Messiah you betrayed and murdered. The Christ has come to you like a message delivered by angels, and your response was to put him to death."

The room fell silent when Stephen finished speaking. As his words took hold, the temple authorities seethed with anger toward him. Stephen remained calm as he stood before the same men who had threatened and beaten Peter and John and had tried and executed Jesus.

He looked up, smiled, and said, "Behold! I see the heavens opening and the Son of Man standing at the right hand of God even now." It was as though Stephen had gone to another place and was no longer the subject of a trial but a guest in the house of God.

One of the rulers of the temple, a young man named Saul, glared at the Christian standing before him. Saul had just been insulted by this defiant Hellenist who dared to suggest that the Pharisees were the ones who had defamed the law of Moses. He voiced his indignation. The high priest nodded and dispatched some of the men in the guard. They ran at Stephen and began to beat him, as the temple court shouted their charges of blasphemy. They dragged Stephen outside the city gate, and Saul gave the order for them to stone Stephen until he was dead.

The temple guards took off their outer garments, laid them at Saul's feet, and began to hurl stones at the young man. Stephen lifted his eyes again to heaven and cried out, just as his Lord Jesus had done in the moment of his own death, "Lord, receive my spirit." And then, falling to his knees, he prayed, "Lord, please do not hold this sin against them."

Then Stephen collapsed on the ground and died as the rocks continued to pelt his body.

Saul left the scene, satisfied that what they had done was for the good of Israel. But the more he considered Stephen's words—during both his trial and his death—the more angry Saul became. How dare this young man, and the sect to which he belonged, question his righteousness. He was a Pharisee among Pharisees who kept God's law to the letter.

Saul presumed that Stephen's resolve and courage was his own—a product of the apostles' teaching and his own desire to be a good disciple. If the Christians' courage was only an overflow of the heart, pressure could break their spirits. And if that didn't work, persecution would crush their inspiration. Either way, Saul resolved to do whatever was in his power to rid his city of the influence of Jesus of Nazareth.

He never considered that those he opposed were part of something God was doing—and that God would be strong for them. Saul thought Gamaliel's wager would prove that these were zealots without roots and that their influence would soon fade, especially now that one of the disciples had paid the same price as Jesus. It was unthinkable to Saul that God would care for them—unthinkable that he had already numbered their days and that man could do nothing to them outside of the perfect, wise will of their Maker.

Stephen's martyrdom was a picture of the substance of his faith. In the face of death he did not despair. Instead he claimed to see the heavens open and the glory of God shining on him. Stephen saw Christ defeat the last enemy in his life, death itself. In his dying moment Stephen experienced the presence of Christ, who was standing at the right hand of God, ready to receive his first martyr and welcome him into eternal life.

During his death Stephen imitated Jesus. As Christ hung on the cross he had cried out to God, "Into your hands I commend my spirit." Stephen prayed the same: "Lord Jesus, receive my spirit." As Jesus was being nailed to the cross he had prayed, "Father, forgive them, they know not what they do." So too, Stephen prayed: "Lord, do not hold this sin against them."

Saul could not understand that Stephen was not relying on the strength of his own zeal to keep his composure during his death. Stephen's courage was not his own. Suffering did not draw from him hopelessness and despair but the imitation of Christ. This was the Holy Spirit's work. The Holy Spirit had acted in Stephen's life in such a way that in his darkest moment, the evidence of Christ's victory over sin and death shone bright like the sun.

Saul did not know what he was up against.

9

PHILIP

Acts 8:2-40

WITHOUT HIS REALIZING IT, Saul's persecution fueled the very thing he was trying to quell.

After he oversaw the stoning death of Stephen, Saul launched a campaign of persecution against the church. He went house to house looking for anyone who followed Jesus, and he dragged them off to prison. His determination to see the church's extinction caused people to leave the area, and with them went the gospel of the risen Christ. As the new Christians scattered throughout Judea and Samaria, so did their message. Gamaliel's words were beginning to ring true: if this was from God, no man could shut it down. No amount of persecution, whether covert or governmentally sanctioned, could tear down what God was building.

The Christian community, rather than keeping silent as Saul and the other temple rulers demanded, honored Stephen's death by picking up the torch he'd laid down. They were beginning to fulfill Jesus' parting words that his people would be his witnesses in Jerusalem, Judea, Samaria, and the uttermost ends of the earth. In the light of Stephen's death and Saul's ensuing persecution, it became soberingly clear that Jesus' people would sometimes be his witnesses in the world through suffering.

Jesus intended for the gospel to spread from Jerusalem to Judea and Samaria. And it did. Persecution served Jesus' Great Commission. Stephen's colaborer in the church, Philip, was one of the men who left Jerusalem because of Saul's persecution. It has long been the way of God to use struggle to shape character, test faith, correct errors, expose sins, and lead his people to places they wouldn't otherwise go. It has long been his way to use difficulty for redemptive purposes. Witnesses to grace are born out of hardship.

Philip was one such witness. Saul's hatred drove him out from his familiar community of faith in Jerusalem into Samaria. But wherever he went, Philip performed signs and wonders and proclaimed the gospel of Jesus Christ, and his message brought great joy to many Samaritans who heard it.

In Samaria there lived a man named Simon, who was a magician. He loved a good display of power, and he loved to show people the illusion of one. People who crave power thrive in a community that craves powerful people, so Simon proclaimed himself to be somebody great. He amazed people with his sorcery and no doubt his exuberance. He was a salesman who gained customers based not on the quality of his product but on the charisma of his personality. People believed he was a great man because he told them he was a great man.

When Philip came to town healing and casting out demons, people began to put their confidence in him because his power seemed even greater than Simon's. Philip preached about Jesus and was persuasive enough that many people trusted in Christ and wanted to be baptized. But others believed only in Philip and the signs and wonders he performed, which was not saving faith. For faith to be saving faith, its object had to be Jesus Christ alone.

The heart of the Samaritans' false belief was that they trusted in signs and wonders, not in Jesus. The experience of their faith was amazement, not humble repentance. Their reason for believing was to gain more power, not to surrender to the lordship of Christ. But many did come to a genuine saving faith. When the apostles in Jerusalem heard that the gospel was beginning to spread throughout Samaria, they sent Peter and John to come down and pray for these new believers to receive the Holy Spirit. They laid hands on those who had been baptized in the name of Jesus, and those people received the Holy Spirit.

When Simon saw what Peter and John were doing, he wanted this power. So he professed faith in Jesus. He wanted to be able to impart the Spirit of God with a touch. He was amazed that Peter and John could do it, and he could picture himself doing this sort of thing too. Simon wanted to wield God's power as his own so that people would revere him. Simon couldn't just be Simon. He needed to be Simon the Great.

So he came to Peter with a handful of money and asked, "How much for that power? Sell me the Holy Spirit so I can use him myself."

Peter saw a man drunk with a lust for power. He said, "Simon, may your silver perish with you because you think you can obtain the gift of God with money. Your heart is not right before God. Repent of your wickedness, Simon. It is killing you. Your hunger for glory has made you a bitter, sick man."

Peter's rebuke caught Simon off guard. The sting of the apostle's words reached his heart. He said, "Sir, please pray for me. Please ask the Lord to spare me from the things you have said so that nothing of what you have said may come upon me."

After ministering there in Simon's town for a while, Peter and John returned to Jerusalem, preaching the gospel to many Samaritan villages along the way. Philip stayed back until the Lord directed him to leave Samaria and head down toward the southern desert. Philip set out on the road to Gaza, leaving a place that was beginning to feel familiar for a destination that was not just foreign but desolate. Nevertheless Philip rose and went, figuring it was better to walk through the desert with Jesus than to live in the streets of familiarity alone.

On the road Philip met a eunuch in a chariot who was traveling home from Jerusalem. He was the treasurer to Candace, the queen of Ethiopia. Eunuchs were male servants in royal households who were emasculated to ensure their loyalty to their post and their right conduct among the women they served. This eunuch was a "God-fearer," a gentile convert to Judaism.

When Philip came upon him the eunuch was studying a scroll—a possession indicating that he was a man of means, power, and education. Philip sensed the Lord prompting him to talk with the eunuch, so he approached the chariot, listening, wondering, and asking the Lord for words. Before he had the opportunity to say anything, he heard the eunuch speaking. He was reading aloud—familiar words from a scroll of the prophet Isaiah. Philip heard the eunuch read,

"Like a sheep he was led to the slaughter
and like a lamb before its shearers is silent,

so he opens not his mouth.

In his humiliation justice was denied him.

Who can describe his generation?

For his life is taken away from the earth."

Philip called out, "Do you understand what you are reading?"

The eunuch stopped the chariot and, by way of invitation, said, "How can I unless someone helps me? Is the prophet referring to himself here, or is he talking about someone else—someone who was yet to come?"

This moment was an opportunity the Lord had been preparing Philip for his entire life. Philip had spent many years studying the Word of God. He read not to complete an assignment but to understand. He knew the books of Moses and the history of the children of Israel. He knew the stories and songs of David and the warnings and invitations to mercy from the prophets. He knew the covenant arc that ran through Scripture since the fall of man in Eden. And now he saw how all of it foreshadowed the coming of Jesus.

Philip offered to help, and the eunuch patted the seat beside him. Philip climbed up, and the two men began to read together. Philip explained how the prophet Isaiah was one of God's heralds who proclaimed the future and coming Messiah who would rescue God's people from their sin by taking the debt of their iniquity upon himself.

The men had a lengthy conversation that traced its way through the whole of Scripture, ending with the story of the life, death, and resurrection of Jesus Christ. Philip and the eunuch made their way from Isaiah to Jesus' Great Commission to make disciples of all the nations, baptizing them in the name of the Father, the Son, and the Holy Spirit.

When the eunuch heard Philip's words, he believed that Jesus was the promised Messiah—Isaiah's slaughtered lamb on whom the Lord laid the iniquity of his people. Was he one of the ones for whom Jesus died? As a eunuch, he was legally forbidden from entering the temple area. As a Gentile, he knew he was not from the line of Abraham. But Isaiah said God had laid upon his suffering servant the iniquity of them all. Did this include him—a Gentile and a eunuch?

As they continued to study Isaiah, they came to a passage that read, "Your seed shall inherit the Gentiles and make the desolate cities to be inhabited." Those whose sin was laid upon Christ included Gentiles.

But what about the exclusion of eunuchs? Even if salvation extended to Gentiles, did it reach so far as to include a Gentile like him? As they read on, they came to another passage in Isaiah that stated, "Let not the foreigner who has joined himself to the Lord say, 'The Lord will surely separate me from his people.' Let not the eunuch say, 'Behold, I am a dry tree.' For thus says the Lord, 'To eunuchs who hold fast to my covenant I will give in my house a monument and a name better than sons and daughters. I will give them an everlasting name that shall not be cut off!'"

When this new disciple from Ethiopia understood that what he was reading was about Christ, that the offer of salvation at so great a price was extended to him, and that he too could be baptized in the name of the triune God, signifying that he belonged to Christ, he said, "Look. Over there is some water. What is to stop me from being baptized right now?"

The eunuch stopped the chariot, and he and Philip went over to the desert stream, where Philip baptized him. The eunuch came out of the water praising God for his mercy and grace and then went on his way. Philip headed east to Azotus on the Mediterranean and preached the resurrection of Jesus there and in all the other towns along the coast as he made his way to his home in Caesarea.

As the message of Jesus spread, so did the number of believers. They were a growing and diverse group made of people from many different races, positions, and religions. Samaritans, Asians, Hebrews, Egyptians, Ethiopians, and others were being persuaded of the truth of the lordship of Jesus Christ. Some came to faith as part of a large crowd responding to a public sermon. Others put their faith in Christ because of a one-on-one conversation. Some were persuaded through signs and wonders, others by way of intellectual ascent. Rich and poor, educated and uneducated, royalty and peasants, men and women, young and old were hearing the message of the risen Christ and the salvation he offered, and the church was growing rapidly, not only in number but in reach.

The church's impact on the region was greater than anyone could have imagined—a fact that only intensified Saul's anger and resolve to snuff them out, even if that meant taking his persecution on the road.

PART 2

PAUL

BEGINS

AD 33–45

10

DAMASCUS ROAD

Acts 9:1-31

*S*AUL'S REPUTATION PRECEDED HIM. Along with rounding up and abusing Christians in Jerusalem, he made sure word spread that he intended not only to arrest Christians but to murder them, as he had done to Stephen. This project of eradicating Christians from the world was not a duty that had been assigned to him. It was his own idea—his passion.

Saul could not be everywhere at once, but he could try to make his presence felt by any who heard his name. He wanted Christians to fear him, so he breathed out threats like a ferocious, panting beast.

In those days Rome ruled the region. One of the ways they governed people of faith was to permit religious leaders to handle religious matters—including legal issues pertaining to the practice of their customs. So Saul went to the high priest in Jerusalem, who had overseen the crucifixion of Jesus, and got written permission to round up any Christian he could find and bring them back to Jerusalem for trial. In those letters Saul the inquisitor was given permission to treat those he arrested as he deemed necessary, even if that meant some would die at his hand.

Saul, letters in hand, set out first to arrest Christians who had fled to the city of Damascus after escaping his net in Jerusalem.

On his way to Damascus, in the middle of the day, an unusually bright light flashed. Saul stopped to look around, his eyes out of focus. Then the light flashed again and again, growing brighter each time until it was brighter than the sun itself. The light blinded Saul and caused him to fall to the ground. As he lay there, blind, he heard a voice say, "Saul, Saul, why are you persecuting me?"

The men who were with Saul had seen him fall, but they had not been blinded by the light he saw. They did not understand what was happening, only that their leader had fallen and looked afraid and confused. But then they heard the voice speaking to Saul, though they saw no one. They were terrified.

Groping for something to hold on to, Saul said, "Who are you, Lord?"

The voice said, "I am Jesus—the one you are persecuting. Get up and go into Damascus. I will tell you what to do once you arrive."

Saul's traveling companions helped him to his feet and led him by the hand into the city. He had been driven to Damascus in the first place by his conviction that the followers of Jesus were a blasphemous band of zealots who needed to be overthrown. But he now entered the city as a man who was himself blind and overthrown—following along as his servants led him by the hand so he could wait on the Lord he had tried to destroy.

For three days Saul sat blind and waiting. During that time he neither ate nor drank. Instead he prayed.

Across town lived a man named Ananias, a follower of Jesus who had been in Jerusalem when the gospel first began to spread. He knew a lot about Saul and his hatred for Christians. He knew Saul wasn't just some raving lunatic. He was a truly dangerous man.

The Lord appeared to Ananias in a vision and said, "Ananias, go over to Straight Street to your friend Judas's house and look for a man from Tarsus called Saul. He is there praying, and I have given him a vision of you. In that vision, you come to him and lay your hands on his eyes and restore his sight."

Ananias felt a chill. He said, "Lord, is this the same man who has been breathing out murderous threats against your followers? I know about him and the evil and pain he has caused your people. And I hear that he is now acting under the authority of the chief priests to arrest and kill those who believe in you. Is this the man you want me to see?"

As far as Ananias was concerned, Saul had come to that city to hunt him. Even if he was blind, he was an enemy—not just of Ananias but of Christ himself. What the Lord was asking him to do did not make sense.

But the Lord said, "Go to him. I have chosen this man to carry my name out into the world—before Gentiles and kings and the children of Israel alike. He will suffer much for my name's sake, but I am preparing him now, and I want you to go to him."

So Ananias went down to the street called Straight, and when he entered Judas's home he found Saul, blind and emptied of venom. Up until the moment he made his presence known, he considered whether to follow through with the Lord's instruction. But when Saul sensed his presence in the room, Ananias knew there was no turning back.

Saul said, "Is someone there?"

Ananias gathered his courage and said, "Brother Saul, the Lord who appeared to you on the road outside the city has also appeared to me. He has sent me to pray for you so that you might regain your sight and receive the Holy Spirit."

Saul winced a little when he heard Ananias call him his brother. Only a few days earlier he would have killed this man. But that wasn't what triggered a reaction in Saul's heart. It was the strange and sudden affection he both felt and received in that moment. He could not fully explain how it happened, but Ananias suddenly seemed more like a friend than an enemy. His brother was speaking to him.

Saul nodded and said, "Please."

As Ananias began to pray, something like scales fell from Saul's eyes, and he was able to see again. Ananias took him to a place where he could be baptized, and he gave him some food, which Saul devoured.

Though Christ's intervention with Saul happened on the Damascus road, that was by no means the whole of Saul's process of conversion. This was a man who had devoted himself to the study of Scripture his entire life. The same words Philip read with the eunuch from Ethiopia, which pointed to the coming Messiah, were hidden deep inside Saul's heart and had been since he was young. Though he had misunderstood and misapplied them, the truth of their meaning could never be emptied. On the road to Damascus, the light of God revealed Saul's blindness and Scripture's brilliance.

His whole life Saul had been a fish caught on the end of the angler's line. He thought he was swimming freely in the waters of his own understanding, but every so often he would feel a tug. Until this moment all he had ever done was fight against it. He did not realize that each time he was being drawn a little closer to the unseen master who had hold of him. There on the

Damascus road, the net wrapped around him, and he was delivered into another life.

After Ananias baptized Saul, the former persecutor began proclaiming the resurrection of Jesus Christ in the synagogues in Damascus. People struggled to believe this was the same man who had done so much violence to the church he now claimed as his own.

Saul remained in that city for the next three years, occasionally travelling to Arabia to study. Throughout this season of his life his message came down to two basic concepts: Jesus was the Son of God, and he was God's only Messiah.

For three years Saul taught about Christ, and his reputation spread. His new passion to proclaim Christ outshone his earlier passion to destroy the church, and because of his ministry, many in Damascus began to put their faith in Jesus. The religious leaders in Damascus regarded Saul as a threat to their work, so they formed a plot to kill him the next time he left the city. They posted watchmen at the city gates day and night to make sure they spotted him the next time he went out. News of this plan made it to some of Saul's friends, who woke him in the middle of the night and told him about the threat. They decided their safest option was to lower Saul over the city wall in a basket under cover of darkness so he could escape to Jerusalem and take refuge with the apostles there.

So Saul left Damascus, and when he arrived in Jerusalem he sent word to the apostles that he wanted to meet with them. They were wary of him—which they had every reason to be. Before Saul's commitment to Christ, he had been committed to ridding the world of Christians—these Christians in particular.

But Barnabas listened to Saul and prayerfully considered what to do. Saul's conversion was as complicated for Barnabas as it was for any of the believers still in Jerusalem. Barnabas would have to personally forgive Saul for the pain and suffering he had caused in order to receive him into their fellowship. Barnabas had felt the heat of the persecution Saul ignited three years back. Some of his close friends had been martyred, others tortured, and others still exiled as the result of Saul's persecution.

Not only did Barnabas need to forgive Saul, he also had to believe in Saul's call to minister the very gospel he had worked so hard to destroy. To defend Saul in front of the apostles meant he would have to feel certain that Saul was not a wolf among the sheep Barnabas loved.

Barnabas spoke with Saul and sought out the genuineness of his faith. He soon was convinced that the God who had raised Jesus from the dead had also given new life to this infamous Pharisee. Barnabas took Saul by the hand and led him before the apostles. He stood as one with Saul, lending his own reputation by affirming God's work in Saul's life before the wary disciples. When Barnabas put his arm around Saul, he wasn't just confirming Saul's calling to the apostles. He was confirming it to Saul too.

The apostles received Saul, and he stayed with Peter for the next two weeks. Late into the night the two men stayed up talking about Jesus. Peter told Saul about the miracle of the loaves and fishes and what it was like to walk on water. Saul told Peter how the Pharisees talked about this mighty little movement. They spoke at length about the central event of their common faith—the crucifixion and resurrection of Jesus Christ.

During those two weeks Saul went into the synagogues and debated the Hellenist religious leaders there. These had been his people. He was one of them. In fact, it was the Hellenistic Jews who'd had Stephen arrested and killed, an event Saul presided over. But now, three years later, Saul stood among his former colleagues, defending with all his heart the doctrine for which he and the others had killed Stephen.

Saul picked up Stephen's torch. This proved to be more than the religious leaders in Jerusalem could bear, so they hatched another plot to kill Saul. After only fifteen days in Jerusalem, Saul once again had to flee.

Before his conversion Saul had chased Christians, persecuting them. As soon as he converted and began to preach Christ, persecution found him, and it didn't find him alone. In Jerusalem, Saul's preaching brought persecution to the entire church—so much that after only two weeks he had to flee. This time he returned to his home city of Tarsus, where he lived in relative obscurity for the next ten years, unknown to the churches in Judea.

Though it would be close to a decade before God would send Barnabas to find Saul and ask him to join him in taking the gospel of Jesus Christ to the Gentile world, the Lord used those ten years to prepare Saul for the work that lay ahead.

During this time the church continued to grow, as did Saul's passion to make Christ known to the world. To better engage with the Gentiles, Saul set aside his Hebrew name and began to go by his Greek name, Paul.

11

WHAT GOD HAS MADE CLEAN

Acts 9:32–10:23

AS PAUL STAYED IN TARSUS, preparing for ministry to the Gentile world, Peter stayed in the vicinity of Jerusalem, attending mainly to the Jewish believers in that area. But as the gospel spread out from Jerusalem, it naturally began to reach parts of the country made up of an increasing number of God-fearing Gentile converts.

Peter began traveling to the various communities of believers that were springing up around Palestine. He wasn't just visiting individual people. Little churches were springing up along Israel's coastline. Philip's journey up the coast saw many come to belief, and news of these young congregations reached Peter, who set out to care for them and instruct them in the faith.

For much of Israel's history, the people's faith had had a geo-graphical epicenter. Before Joshua's conquest it was the traveling tabernacle, and after Israel took Canaan it was Jerusalem. But after

Pentecost, Jesus' disciples came to understand what Jesus had meant when he told the Samaritan woman that the time was coming when people would no longer gather at a temple to find God but would worship in spirit and in truth. It wasn't that the temple of the Lord was no longer necessary. It was that the temple of the Lord had shifted from being a structure made of stone and wood to a people made of flesh and bone. He would no longer inhabit an ark but the human heart. His presence would move out into the world through living stones, temples of the Holy Spirit. These temples would be all those people who believed in Jesus as their Christ.

Accepting this shift did not happen overnight. Jerusalem had always been the seat of spiritual vitality. It had been a destination for obedient pilgrims. For generations, people had come to that city to worship because God had commanded them to. But now, the gospel was spreading out from Jerusalem, and the disciples' objective was not to gather these new Christ-followers in Jerusalem but to see them continue to spread as Jesus had commissioned them—taking the message of salvation beyond Jerusalem to Judea, Samaria, and the ends of the earth.

On his way to the coast Peter passed through a village called Lydda, where he met a man named Aeneas who had been bedridden for eight years. Seeing him, Peter said, "Aeneas, Jesus Christ heals you. Get up and take your bed with you."

Immediately Aeneas felt the sensation return to his legs, and he stood. He stooped over, picked up his mat, and walked around, testing his new stability.

Aeneas, as with the beggar at the gate called Beautiful in Jerusalem, was known in his community for his affliction. As soon as

people saw him restored and learned that the apostle Peter had
healed him in the name of Jesus, many of the residents of Lydda and
the entire coastal plain region of Sharon turned to the Lord. With
Peter came a revival.

Believers in nearby Joppa heard that Peter was in Lydda. They
sent an urgent message asking him to come. One of their sisters in
Christ, a seamstress named Tabitha, had died. Tabitha had a reputation similar to that of Barnabas. She was full of good works, generosity, and kindness. She was a source of strength and encouragement for many, and they felt her death as a heavy loss.

When Peter arrived in Joppa, Tabitha's grieving friends came out
to take him to the room where she lay. Several widows from the
community came to Peter in tears, showing him garments she had
made while she was alive. They held the articles with affection, as
though the tunics Tabitha had made were an extension of the
woman herself—the work of her hands. They showed Peter the care
she took in her craft—the seams, the color of the fabric, the beauty
of her art. And they wept for her.

These women loved Tabitha, and they missed her. They wanted
Peter to do something about it.

Peter had been in a room like this before. Several years earlier,
he and James and John had gone with Jesus to the home of a man
named Jairus, a ruler in the synagogue in Capernaum. Jairus's
daughter, Talitha, had just died, and Peter followed Jesus into a
room that was, for Jairus and his wife, the saddest place in the
world—the room where their little girl's body lay dead.

Peter, James, and John had looked on as Jesus took Talitha's hand
and whispered into her ear, "Honey, get up." They watched in total
astonishment as the little girl sat up and began looking around the
room, as though she had just awoken from a deep sleep.

When Peter saw Tabitha lying as Talitha had, he sent everyone out of the room. Then he knelt down beside her and prayed, remembering the way his friend Jesus had loved Jairus's family so well. Looking at the dead woman, Peter said, "Tabitha, arise." As soon as he spoke, life came back into her body, and she sat up, looking at Peter.

Peter smiled at the woman and offered her his hand, which she took. He helped Tabitha to her feet and led her out to where her friends and family were waiting and praying. When they saw her alive they began to weep and praise God for his mercy and kindness to them.

The church continued to grow as people heard the stories of Tabitha and Aeneas.

The apostles performed many wonders in those days. Those miracles served a function. God worked wonders through his apostles so that those listening could know with confidence that these men were appointed by God, as evidenced through signs. This validation was crucial because the apostles were the ones appointed by Christ to instruct the church in sound doctrine. It was Jesus himself who gathered his twelve apostles to give them the authority to preach. They were set apart for this work.

Signs and wonders authenticated the apostles' message, and many who witnessed or heard about the signs and wonders put their faith in Jesus. After Aeneas was healed, people turned to the Lord. After Tabitha was raised from the dead, many believed in Jesus Christ. Though Peter's miracles validated his message, they did not point to the power of Peter. They pointed to the power of Christ. Jesus was the one people put their faith in. Jesus was the one people wanted to know.

Up the coast from Joppa, in Caesarea, there was a Roman centurion named Cornelius. Cornelius was a man of prayer and generosity who cared for the needs of those in his community. As a God-fearing Gentile who followed the Lord but had not converted to Judaism, Cornelius was not quite an outsider to Judaism, but neither was he an insider. He lived in two worlds—the religious world of the children of Abraham and the civil world of Caesar's Rome.

One afternoon while he was praying, he saw a vision of an angel of the Lord. The centurion fell to the floor in terror as the angel spoke his name, "Cornelius."

Daring not to lift his head, Cornelius said, "Yes, Lord."

The angel said, "The Lord God has heard your prayers. He has seen your generosity and counted it as done unto him. Send some of your men to Joppa. There is a man there named Simon Peter. He is staying with a tanner named Simon who lives beside the sea. Have your men bring him to you."

Cornelius summoned two of his personal servants and one of his soldiers—a man he knew also feared the Lord—and he told them about his vision and sent them down the coast to Joppa to find Peter at Simon the tanner's house.

The next day, as Cornelius's men made their way to Joppa, Peter went up onto Simon's roof and began to pray. It was noon, and Peter was hungry, but Simon's wife was still preparing the meal. As he waited on the roof and prayed, Peter fell into a sort of trance and saw a vision. Peter saw the Lord lower a sheet filled with all manner of clean and unclean animals, reptiles, and birds. The Lord told Peter to get up and take and eat.

Thinking this was a test, Peter said, "Never, Lord. I have never eaten anything unclean. I have not yet defiled myself in that way, and I will not."

The Lord said, "Do not call unclean what I have made clean."

This conversation happened three times before the sheet was again lifted up into the heavens.

Peter did not immediately understand the meaning of the vision. It confused him. But soon after the sheet of clean and unclean animals was taken back up into heaven, the Holy Spirit told Peter three men were there looking for him and that he should go with them immediately because the Lord himself had sent them.

At that moment Cornelius's men arrived at Simon's house and asked for Peter. Peter came down and said, "I'm the one you're looking for. Why have you come?"

The soldier told Peter about Cornelius's vision and how the voice from heaven had told him to send for Peter so his household might hear what Peter had to say.

Since Jesus' resurrection, Gentiles had heard and believed the gospel. And it was generally assumed that a Gentile's conversion to Christ included some manner of conversion to Judaism—if not in name, at least in custom. When Gentiles came to Christ, they came by way of Jewish leaders. But Cornelius's invitation was the first time Peter had been summoned to go to Gentiles alone. The spread of the gospel was not just geographical; it was also ethnic.

Peter had grown up in a culture where Jews and Gentiles were separate—the clean did not associate with the unclean. Though he was a leader of the church, Peter was still very much a student of the Lord. And as it has always been, a true student often has to do as much unlearning as learning. Peter had elitist tendencies woven into his thinking, and it would take time for him to learn this was no way for a Christian to live.

When the Lord lowered the sheet of unclean animals and told Peter to eat, he was telling Peter that Christ alone made a thing clean—nothing else. The lesson for Peter was that the Lord did not consider the Gentiles to be unclean and neither must he. He had to learn to see beyond his partiality. He could not call common what God cherished. He had to love what the Lord loved.

After listening to what Cornelius's men had to say, Peter invited them to spend the night. In the morning they set out together for Caesarea to meet Cornelius and see what the Lord intended to do there.

12

A ROOM FULL
OF GENTILES

Acts 10:24–11:18

W HEN PETER CAME TO CORNELIUS'S HOUSE, he was the foreigner. He was a Jew. Cornelius and his family were Gentiles.
But God had been preparing them both for this meeting. Peter was
beginning to recognize a pattern: the Lord prepared people's hearts
to hear the gospel, and he also prepared his servants to proclaim it.
The Lord prepared Cornelius for Peter by telling him Peter had a
message he was commanded by God to preach. And the Lord told
Peter to speak because the message he had been commanded to
preach was the one the world needed to hear.

As Peter and some of the believers from Joppa neared Caesarea,
one of Cornelius's men ran ahead to let him know they were close.
Cornelius gathered his family and some friends to wait together.
When Peter entered Cornelius's house, the Roman centurion, whose

life was pledged to the service of Caesar, fell at Peter's feet and
began to worship him.

Immediately Peter took Cornelius by the hand and said, "Stand
up, sir. I am just a man like you. Do not worship me."

Cornelius apologized and led Peter into the next room, where a
small crowd had gathered. Peter looked around the house filled
with Gentiles, many of whom appeared to be genuinely surprised
that this Jewish man had actually come to be with them.

Peter said, "You know the law that says it is not right for a Jew
to associate with people of other nations. But God has shown me
that I should not regard any person as unclean, or somehow less of
a man. So when Cornelius's men found me I came without hesi-
tation. Now, why did you send for me?"

Cornelius told Peter about his vision—how the Lord knew about
Cornelius's desire to walk with God and how the Lord had told him
to send men to Joppa to find Peter so that they might hear all that
the Lord had commanded the apostle to teach.

The fact that Cornelius's vision had been accurate—that there
was a man named Peter who was, in fact, staying at Simon the tanner's house—was enough to raise the curiosity of everyone present.
So they all looked at Peter and waited for him to speak.

Peter stood and said, "Here is what I know: God shows no partiality."

Though he stood in a room full of Gentiles, as soon as he began
to preach, what separated them faded to the background, and what
united them came to the front.

Peter focused on humanity's need for peace with God, which
could only come through Jesus Christ. Peter's thesis, that mankind
could have peace with God through Jesus Christ, was incompre-
hensibly good news because, to a man, no one knew perfect peace
with God on their own.

Though Peter was proclaiming the gospel to people who were culturally and religiously different from him, peace with God was not a concept unique to Jewish thought. Every person in the room knew that things in this world were not as they were meant to be. Peace with God was good news because mankind was created to relate to God in a more intimate, face-to-face way than any other created thing.

Peter explained that humanity's relationship with God had been fractured by sin, and try as they might they could never make themselves clean. Without Christ they were separated from God. There was no peace. Through faith in Christ, however, they were not only rejoined to God; they were cleansed of all their sin. All that was wrong would be put right.

This message of peace had universal appeal. Every generation and place on the globe has felt the reality of sadness and frustration. All of humanity has lamented the absence of peace, hope, and goodness. The promise of peace with God didn't just address a Jewish problem. It addressed a human problem—separation from God.

Peter moved from proclaiming peace with God to focusing on the significance of the baptism of Jesus. This was significant because at Jesus' baptism God declared that Jesus was his Son—the one who came bearing the message Cornelius and his friends and family needed to hear. When Jesus was baptized the Holy Spirit descended on him, setting him apart for the work he was sent to do. Jesus' baptism authenticated his lordship over all. Jesus' authority to give his people peace with God was not given to him by man but by the Father himself. Those who needed to be reconciled to God had been given a reconciler by God.

As Peter explained this to Cornelius's household, they began to see the reach of Christ's redemption and how it extended beyond ethnic

Israel to all of humanity. Peter laid out the essential facts of the gospel necessary for faith in Christ—the fact of his life, the fact of his death on the cross, and the fact of his resurrection from the dead. Jesus' sinless life and death in their place and his resurrection accomplished God's plan of salvation. By rising from the grave Jesus broke the power of death's hold over them by paying the wage of sin—death—only to reclaim his life, which he gives to all who believe. Jesus was the one appointed by God to judge the living and the dead.

After explaining all this, Peter appealed for those listening to believe, saying, "Everyone who believes in him receives forgiveness of sins through his name."

While he was speaking, the Spirit of God came on those who were listening. It was just like what had happened in Jerusalem at Pentecost. In that moment at Cornelius's house, the Holy Spirit descended on the people gathered, and as it had happened in Jerusalem, the people began to speak in other tongues.

The Lord was working among the Gentiles in the same exact way he had among the Jews—even among the apostles themselves. Peter and those who had come with him were amazed at what was happening. These Gentiles received the Holy Spirit when they believed in Christ, and not one of them converted to Judaism first.

Peter said, "Is there anyone here who doubts the authenticity of this conversion we've just witnessed? They have received the Holy Spirit just like we did. Let us baptize them with water too."

Cornelius and his household were baptized. They took on themselves the outward visible sign of belonging to the church. Peter was still learning, but he had come to believe that Gentiles could be saved without first converting to Judaism. He believed it because he witnessed it, and it astonished him. God was continually expanding Peter's understanding of the breadth and scope of his saving grace. It all came down to the one basic need every single person who has ever lived shares—the need for peace with their Maker, which was accomplished through Jesus Christ alone.

Over the next several months, word of what happened at Cornelius's house spread. People were amazed to hear how the Holy Spirit had come to Gentiles in the same way he had to Jews. The conversion of Cornelius's household caused such a stir that many sought out witnesses who were there so they could hear the story firsthand. God was transforming lives and extending his grace to all manner of people from every corner of the world.

In those days, Peter, Barnabas, Phillip, and hundreds of other believers were ministering throughout the region, testing the reach of the gospel. Through their hands God healed. Through their words God converted. Through their prayers God intervened. And through their suffering God carried on with the steady work of building his church.

But a group that came to be known as the circumcision party couldn't believe that God would show this sort of grace to Gentiles. How could God consider the two equals? Surely he would at least require Gentiles to convert to Judaism first.

Peter responded to his critics not by rebuking them for questioning his apostolic authority but by giving a humble, precise description of what had happened. Peter understood that what God did in Caesarea was unexpected. It surprised even Peter, who also had to learn this new paradigm that in Christ there was no distinction between Jew and Gentile. Not only were people able to come to Christ without first converting to Judaism; there was only one church to which both Jews and Gentiles belonged. Neither group would have predicted this sort of unity in Christ, but it was what they had.

Peter said to members of the circumcision party, "Look. If God gave the same gift to Gentiles as he gave to us when we first believed in the Lord Jesus Christ, who am I that I should try to stand in God's way? All I can tell you is that it happened. I was there. I am a witness to the fact that their conversion is real and so is their faith."

Peter's evidence made the prosecution rest, at least for a while. Some among them would revert again to this idea that Gentiles needed to convert to Judaism in order to be saved. But at least on this occasion when they heard Peter they were persuaded, and they gave glory to God for what he had done.

They could not dispute the apparent fact that the Lord had done something beyond their wildest imaginations by reaching out to people not like them. It seemed criminal that it was so easy for Gentiles like Cornelius to come to the same faith that members of the circumcision party had worked for so long to follow. They obeyed all the rules, making sure the unclean world of the Gentiles didn't defile them. Had it all been for nothing?

Deep down the circumcision party wasn't primarily upset with Peter or the Gentiles. It was God who offended them. They prided themselves on thinking they had managed to earn a measure of God's favor through their effort—through all the laws they had kept, all the defilements they had kept themselves from, and all the piety they had displayed. The idea that God's grace and kindness could be unmerited was not just incomprehensible. It was offensive.

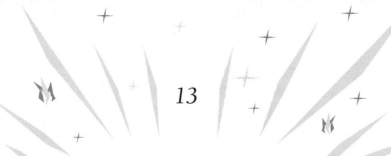

13

BARNABAS AND PAUL IN ANTIOCH

Acts 11:19-30

W*HILE PERSECUTION WAS DRIVING BELIEVERS*—and the gospel—to far-flung communities outside of Jerusalem, and while Paul was in Tarsus preparing for ministry, Barnabas stayed in Jerusalem with the apostles. He wanted to be with them as they weathered oppression from the temple authorities. He was devoted to his brothers and sisters there, and he did not want to leave them in their season of suffering. So he stayed in the hotbed of persecution.

Some Christians from Cyprus and Cyrene came to the city of Antioch and preached about the risen Christ to the Hellenists there. A great number of people put their faith in Jesus, and when reports reached the apostles in Jerusalem that the church was growing rapidly, they realized that they needed to provide some sort of theological oversight and care. Antioch was home to half a million people. It was the third-largest city in the Roman Empire after

Rome and Alexandria, and its vibrant, growing body of believers needed a shepherd.

The apostles came to their dear friend Barnabas and asked if he would go. Barnabas agreed. He was a good pastor. His reputation as an encourager preceded him. And the people of Antioch came to know him as a good man who was full of the Holy Spirit.

Barnabas was guileless. He carried no air of superiority. When he arrived in Antioch and saw the grace of God defining this community of believers, he felt genuine gratitude to Christ. He was glad to be with them, and the church grew under his care. But soon the Christian community grew too large for him to lead on his own. So he decided to travel to Tarsus to see if he could find some help.

In Tarsus Barnabas asked around until he found the house he was looking for. When he knocked, the door opened, and there stood Paul. The two men regarded each other for a moment before Barnabas broke into a smile and threw his arms around Paul's neck. The affection they felt for one another was genuine. In his past Paul had played a role in murdering one of Barnabas's closest friends, Stephen, so these men had to build their friendship on the saving grace of God. Otherwise they would both be hopeless. There was no room in their relationship for bitterness or hate. They were not driven by their pasts but by the eternal road that lay ahead of them both—a road that they would walk together if only for a season.

Paul welcomed Barnabas, and Barnabas told Paul how the gospel had continued to spread. He described how Gentiles were now converting as well, without having to convert to Judaism. Then Barnabas told Paul about what was happening in the great city of Antioch.

"I need your help," Barnabas said. "Come lead with me."

It had been close to thirteen years since Paul's conversion on the road to Damascus, and he had spent that time learning from the Lord and ministering in his community. But the Lord was calling him to something else—to leave and go to the place the Lord would show him. He packed his belongings like a man who did not expect to come home anytime soon, and he and Barnabas set out for Antioch.

Paul and Barnabas spent the next full year in that city—teaching, leading, and caring for an ever-growing church, which consisted mostly of Gentile believers. It was one of Barnabas's wisest acts of humility to search out Paul and ask him to help him in Antioch. Through this partnership their joys were doubled and their burdens cut in half. The Lord grabbed the attention of the watching world, leaving those around them looking for a name by which to call these peculiar people. During this time, people began referring to followers of Jesus as "Christians."

While Paul and Barnabas were in Antioch, a God-fearing man from Jerusalem named Agabus came to them and said the Holy Spirit had told him of a great coming famine. Agabus believed the famine would take place before the end of the Roman Emperor Claudius's reign.

Roman emperors' reigns could not be counted on to last for very long, and with Claudius now into his fifth year, Barnabas and Paul sensed the urgency in Agabus's report. Though there never came an empire-wide famine during Claudius's rule, there were many localized famines, one of which hit Judea and the city of Jerusalem.

Barnabas and Paul gathered the church and told them of the coming famine, noting that it had possibly already begun. When the Christians in Antioch—a wealthy Gentile city—heard about the need of the Jewish believers in Jerusalem, each person gave what they could. Then they sent Barnabas and Paul to personally deliver the relief they had collected. The world had seldom heard of such charity—one race of people collecting money to help another.

Though the Gentiles' history with the Jews in Jerusalem was often strained, for the believers in Antioch, the Christians in Jerusalem were brothers and sisters. What the world had long divided the Lord had brought together.

Not everyone received this fledgling unity between Jews in Jerusalem and Gentiles in Antioch with joy. The temple authorities in Jerusalem still wanted to see Jesus' influence come to an end so they could be rid of the nuisance of all the converts to Christ and their newfound zeal for the church.

The religious leaders had learned a long time ago that Rome could be a useful tool in dealing with their problems. The Roman governors had been charged with the work of collecting taxes and maintaining order—both of which they delegated to the Jewish leaders of the land. If the religious leaders could ensure that taxes were paid and the people respected Rome's authority, the governors would work to make their cohabitation as peaceful as possible.

The Roman governors had a vested interest in peace as well because it helped them look capable in the eyes of those who had the power to promote them. If they could not maintain peace in their present situations, those over them would be reticent to give them any more power.

The religious leaders in Jerusalem picked up on this quandary and exploited it to get the Roman governors to cater to them. Around the time of the famine, the temple authorities began to voice their displeasure with the Christians to their governor, Herod Agrippa I. Herod Agrippa I was the grandson of Herod the Great. Like his grandfather, Agrippa was a builder who worked to see his territory expand. Before long, he had managed to acquire a provincial kingdom almost as large as Herod the Great's. He who has much has much to lose.

The temple authorities came to Agrippa, complaining about their problem with Christians, insinuating that this new influential sect represented a failure on Rome's part to properly execute a man. The Christian community, if not held in check, could one day grow to become a resistance army. What was Herod prepared to do about that? the temple rulers wondered.

Peter, James, and John, along with the other apostles, continued to teach and minister in Jerusalem. As the church grew, so did their reputations as men who had not only known Jesus of Nazareth before his crucifixion and resurrection but had been his closest friends. Peter, James, and John were brothers in the faith and friends since they were young. They carried themselves with authority and grace—each having known the kindness of Jesus in the face of their respective failures to stand with him in his darkest hour.

When Barnabas and Paul arrived in Jerusalem with the gift from the Christians in Antioch, the apostles took them in—thrilled to see their old friend Barnabas and eager to spend time with Paul. For his part, Paul was also eager to listen to the apostles' stories about Jesus and to learn from them.

Many nights these men sat up with Paul trading stories and re-membering their days with Jesus in Galilee and Judea. James told Paul and Barnabas how Jesus and the disciples had been traveling through Samaria one day when they came to a town that clearly did not want them there. James and John took exception to this lack of hospitality and said to Jesus, "Lord, do you want us to call down fire from heaven to consume this place?"

On another occasion he and John had sent their mother to take Jesus aside and ask on their behalf if Jesus would let her boys sit at his right and his left in heaven. When the other disciples found out about this later, they were indignant. But James and John were known for this sort of behavior. Their zeal went out before them even when they were naïve about their own limits.

James saw it as a wonder that Jesus didn't cut him loose for all his arrogance. What he did instead was bring to bear the truth of who these men were. Jesus gave these brothers a nickname that reflected their passion—the Sons of Thunder. And he kept them around because he wanted them around.

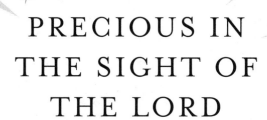

14

PRECIOUS IN
THE SIGHT OF
THE LORD

Acts 12:1-25

N*O ONE KNOWS FOR CERTAIN THE HOUR* of their death. Not long after Jesus' resurrection, he appeared to his disciples on the shore of Galilee. Peter and the other disciples were fishing. When Peter, who had only days earlier denied knowing Jesus, recognized his risen Lord standing on the banks, he jumped out of the boat and swam to shore so he could fall at the feet of this friend he'd betrayed.

As Peter wept at the feet of his Lord, Jesus asked Peter if he loved him. Peter could only give one answer—the true one: yes, he loved Jesus. He had denied knowing Jesus, but he loved him. He was a walking contradiction, but he was loved and kept by the grace of God.

Jesus told Peter then that he would grow old. His eyes would dim, and he would be led by the hand to places he did not want to go. This was how Jesus predicted that Peter would die as a martyr for his faith.

Peter looked at John who, with his brother James, had been with Jesus since the start, and said, "What about him? Will he follow the same fate?"

Jesus said, "What is that to you? I am telling you your story. If he lives until I return, that is not your concern. Your call is to follow me."

Reports of this conversation spread, and many interpreted it as Jesus saying John would not die. But John, Peter, James, and the others knew this was not what Jesus meant. Jesus had already told James and John earlier that they would drink from the same crucible as their Lord. All they knew was that they would each probably die as martyrs and that their deaths were already known and precious in the sight of the Lord.

This did not make the prospect of laying down their lives for Jesus any easier, but as Peter had once said, where else could they go? Jesus alone had the words of life.

About a decade after the resurrection, Peter, James, and John were leading the church in Jerusalem. They had become the public faces of Christianity within Jerusalem and beyond. In some people's minds this made them heroes. For others they were targets.

Herod Agrippa knew that with every passing month the religious leaders in Jerusalem were becoming harder and harder to please. He resented the idea that he would have to owe them anything, but a current of unrest ran below the surface of the religious community in his capital city, and he knew that at the heart of it lay a growing tension between the temple authorities and the growing community of Christians who did not seem to need the religion the Sanhedrin offered.

Herod decided it might be time for a gesture of goodwill to the religious leaders, so he arrested James, John's brother, and several other Christians in the city. Herod beat many of them, but he brought James to his court for a trial.

A story later circulated that when James was brought to Herod, the soldier who led him heard James's testimony about Jesus and was moved to confess to Herod that he too had become a Christian. Both men, as the story went, were then led away to be executed together. On their way to the sword, the soldier asked James to forgive him for his part in what was happening. James considered the man for a moment and kissed him and said, "Be at peace." Then the two men were beheaded together.

James's death meant nothing to Herod. It was little more than an experiment. Herod wanted to see how the temple authorities would respond. When he saw that James's death pleased the Sanhedrin, he decided to do it again. He arrested Peter and put him in jail during the Feast of the Unleavened Bread. Herod figured he could really please the religious leaders if he presented the apostle Peter for trial during Passover, just as Pilate had done with Jesus. That was his plan—to hold Peter until Passover and make his trial a public spectacle.

Four squads of soldiers—sixteen men in all—guarded Peter's cell in the Antonia Fortress in Jerusalem. Herod's allocation of manpower indicated that he saw Peter as a threat to peace. It was hard to overstate the impact the church was having on Jerusalem. Christianity was unraveling the social fabric of the Jewish way of life, and every time someone tried to snuff it out, it only spread and grew stronger—sometimes winning over those who opposed it the most. Peter led this movement, and with each arrest and beating, his voice became more authoritative and his circle of friends larger. He was becoming the prototypical revolutionary. Peter was a paradox, feared by his captors who were about to kill him.

On the night before his trial, which would certainly lead to his death, Peter slept soundly. So soundly, in fact, that he did not notice the luminous angel who appeared at his side in his cell. The angel poked Peter to wake him as a mother wakes a sleeping child. Peter stirred, still groggy, and the angel told him to get dressed and to gather his things. They were leaving.

The chains that bound Peter to the two guards fell off. The angel put the guards into a deep sleep, and they did not wake as the cell door opened and Peter and the angel stepped out into the hall. The angel led Peter through the series of gates that eventually led to the street. Peter was still shaking off the confusion of sleep as he followed. The angel vanished as the last gate swung open on its own. Peter stepped into the street, alone and free. When he realized he was actually standing outside the prison, he was suddenly aware that this was not a dream. God had delivered him.

Many in the church had gathered at the home of Mary, the mother of John Mark, who was Barnabas's cousin, praying earnestly for Peter. They held little hope that his coming trial would end with release, so they prayed that Peter would die well. These were informed prayers. When Jesus was arrested by the Romans to please the Jews, he was crucified. When James was arrested by the Romans to please the Jews, he was beheaded. Why would it be any different for Peter?

When the sun came up to mark the end of Passover, Peter's trial would commence, and he would die—the Christians gathered at Mary's house were certain of this. Still, they prayed deep into the night asking for the Lord to intervene.

After making his way through the shadowy streets of the sleeping city, Peter arrived at Mary's house. The lights were still on, and he could hear those inside praying. It was only a few hours until dawn, but they were still up, united in hearts and minds, praying to God for Peter.

Peter knocked on the door. A servant girl named Rhoda asked through the closed door, "Who's there?"

"It's me. Peter."

Rhoda stepped back in terror. She recognized Peter's voice. Leaving him standing outside, she ran into the room where everyone had gathered and told them Peter was at the door. They told Rhoda she was out of her mind, but she insisted. The room went cold. They wondered if Peter had already been executed and standing at the door was Peter's ghost.

They heard him knock again. Mary and John Mark opened the door to find Peter very much alive. They surrounded him and began to praise God. Peter raised his hands and told them to quiet down so they wouldn't wake the neighbors, and then he told them about how the angel had appeared in his cell to wake him and led him out into the streets before disappearing. Peter told them to pass this story along to Jesus' brother James and to the other disciples. Then he left and hid out in another place.

It is a fearful thing to fall into the hands of the living God. That morning, the guards awoke to find Peter missing. They searched for him but could not find him. When they reported the mysterious escape, Herod widened the hunt but could not find the missing apostle. The angel of the Lord released Peter and no one, including the two guards chained to him, knew how. This infuriated Herod, not just because it appeared that his guards were incompetent but because events like this made rulers look incompetent too. So Herod had Peter's guards executed.

This was a tragedy for all who heard it, and it was ultimately Herod's own fault. Because James's death had curried favor with the Jews, Herod had marked Peter for death as well. Because the angel rescued Peter, four—or maybe all sixteen—of Peter's guards were put to death. And Peter was now on the run.

After Herod executed Peter's guards, he left for the coastal city of Caesarea for a festival held there in Caesar's honor. Time away from the tensions in Jerusalem might have done him some good were it not for the fact that Herod was also struggling with his northern neighbors, Tyre and Sidon. These cities depended on Judea for food, so peace with Herod was essential for survival. But they had done some things that upset him, and they knew he was not pleased with them. So when they heard he was in nearby Caesarea, leaders from Tyre and Sidon sought an audience with the king through Herod's trusted personal servant, Blastus. Their agenda was to beg for peace.

Herod granted the meeting. When the day arrived, he set up the throne room to be as intimidating as possible. His robes were woven with silver so that when he entered the theater at daybreak the sun radiated off of him in a glorious array of light that inspired fear in everyone who saw him. In the most imposing, resplendent regalia only a mighty king with the power to crush his enemies could afford, Herod made sure the emissaries of Tyre and Sidon understood that peace with him required nothing short of worship.

The people of Tyre and Sidon, dependent on this king for their survival, responded with great fear and flattery. They lifted their voices, saying, "You are more than a mortal king! You are a god!"

Herod received their praise and spoke to them as though he were a god. He chided, threatened, and welcomed into his protection any who would remember their proper place before him. As he spoke, they praised him even more, saying even his voice was the voice of a god.

Though a humble king would have put a stop to their flattery, Herod drank it in. But as he stood in his silver robe with beams of light radiating out from his body, he looked up and saw an owl perched on a rope above him. Herod was a superstitious man. When he saw the owl he feared it was a bad omen—a warning from God that only he should be worshiped. But before he could deflect the crowd's praise, a pain shot through his abdomen and up into his heart, and he collapsed to the ground.

His attendants ran to his side and picked up the fallen king and took him into his chamber, where five days later he died of complications from an infestation of intestinal worms.

The angel of the Lord struck down Herod Agrippa because he didn't give God glory. Instead he received it for himself. His death was a reminder that God held the power to strike someone dead where they stood, just as he had the authority to command a worm to take up residence in the bowel of a king at such a time that later, at the precise moment when the king was accepting praises due to God alone, the worm outgrew its confines and caused such pain in its host that the king had to be carried to his bed where he lay until dead.

Much devastation had been wrought by the whims of this dying tetrarch. James was dead, and his brother John and everyone else close to him were stricken with grief. Peter had to sit and wait in Herod's prison during the Passover, a holy feast that celebrated how God had liberated his people from tyranny. And though an angel miraculously released him, he had to immediately go into hiding. This was Herod's mess. He made mothers mourn, friends weep, brothers grieve, and children fear. But though he acted with impunity, unmovable and swift, he was never in control.

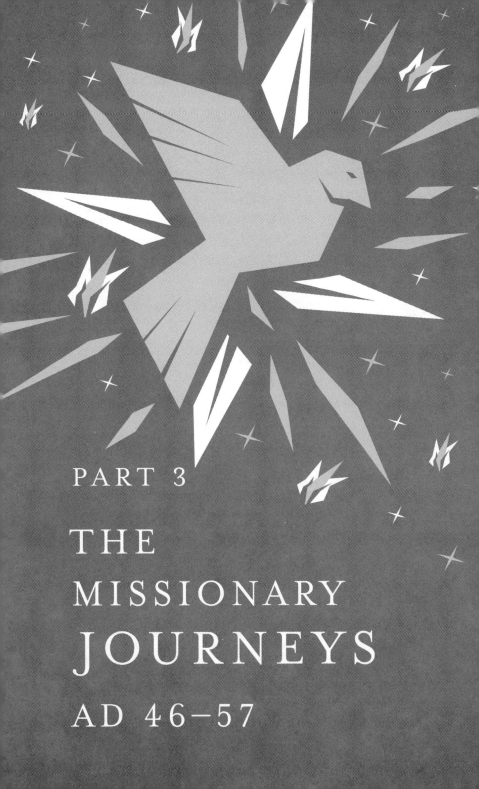

PART 3

THE
MISSIONARY
JOURNEYS
AD 46–57

15

A DIVERSE
AND SENDING
CHURCH

Acts 13:1-52

A S OMINOUS AS HEROD MUST have been, he was just a man. His attempt to derail the church amounted to less than a child trying to take down a lion with a pebble. This ruler who appeared so powerful was gone in a moment, but the Word of God stood. Though many tried to destroy it, twist it, or profit from it, the gospel never folded. After Herod collapsed before the delegates of Tyre and Sidon, the Word of God continued to increase and multiply, and the Christians were emboldened to continue preaching. No matter what people of power intended to do to them, these apostles seemed to be immortal until it was the will of God for them to die.

Barnabas and Paul returned to Antioch from Jerusalem and brought with them John Mark, Barnabas's cousin. Having been sobered by the death of James, inspired by the release of Peter, and emboldened by the death of Herod, they had a rekindled fire in their hearts for the spread of the gospel. The leaders of the church in Antioch, Barnabas and Paul included, gathered to pray, fast, worship, and seek the face of God.

The church in Antioch had proven itself strong in the faith, taking it upon itself to collect an offering for famine relief in Jerusalem. They sent Barnabas and Paul to deliver it. Their leadership was diverse, made up of Africans (Simeon and Lucius), Jews (Barnabas and Paul), and a Roman who was raised with Herod (Manaen). They had their sights set on the furthest reaches of the earth because their leadership had come from far-reaching places themselves.

The Christians in Antioch believed the Great Commission extended to them, and they wanted God to make his purpose plain. They asked the Lord if they should be the ones to take the gospel of Jesus even further. They had many questions. Should they go now? Whom should they send? Should they send their own teachers? There was no precedent for this. No one had ever attempted this sort of world mission. They sought the Holy Spirit's counsel because they knew they were being called to something.

They fasted and prayed, asking how Christ would use them. The Holy Spirit told them to set apart Barnabas and Paul for the work God had prepared. This required courage. God was calling them to release two of their best leaders into the world with no guarantee of their return. Obedience like this would test their character; it meant a chapter in their story was coming to a close. There was a cost to following Jesus. It was God's prerogative to rearrange the stage.

The church's response showed signs of great spiritual health. They gathered around these dearly loved brothers, laid their hands on them, blessed them, and sent them off as God's ambassadors on their first missionary journey.

A subtle shift occurred during this first missionary journey—
Barnabas and Paul became Paul and Barnabas. Paul took the lead,
and Barnabas yielded it to him without complaint or wounded ego.
God's call on Paul's life as the apostle to the Gentiles was underway.
When Paul took the lead, it revealed the true nature of Barnabas's
leadership. Barnabas had been the first to really believe in Paul's call.
Before the apostles in Jerusalem, Barnabas argued for Paul's credi-
bility and won the brothers over. Ten years later he went and found
Paul in Tarsus and brought him to Antioch, all the while serving as
Paul's mentor. But all this time, Barnabas knew that God's call on
Paul's life was special.

Barnabas's primary hunger was not for position or recognition but
for God's glory to be seen throughout Rome. Barnabas understood
that God had a plan to bring the gospel to the Gentile world—to
Barnabas's world. And he knew Paul was meant to lead that mission.
Barnabas wasn't merely a character in his own story, or in Paul's story.
He was in the middle of God's story, and God alone was the hero, the
leader, the lover, and the Savior of the world Barnabas inhabited.

As a chapter in the life of the church in Antioch came to a close,
another chapter began. Paul and Barnabas traveled to Cyprus, an
island in the Mediterranean and Barnabas's original home. They
arrived with a simple plan—to start at the eastern port of Salamis
and traverse the island ninety miles to the western port of Paphos.
They stopped in villages along the way to preach in the synagogues
and then to the Gentiles. This would become their pattern: to the
Jew first and then to the Gentile.

As they traveled, their message went on ahead of them. When
they arrived at Paphos, the proconsul, the acting Roman magistrate

of the Island, wanted to hear what they had to say. He was an educated man, and he was open to hearing the gospel. There was a
problem, however. The proconsul had a counselor, a magician
named Elymus, whose livelihood depended on payment from the
proconsul. When Elymus heard the apostles' message of the exclu-
sivity of faith in Christ alone, he pulled the proconsul aside and
tried to persuade him away from the faith. He didn't want the proconsul to believe in Christ because he wanted the proconsul to trust
him only.

When Paul learned of Elymus's motives, he stared straight into
the sorcerer's eyes and rebuked him with the authority of the Holy
Spirit. Elymus was the son of the devil, Paul said, full of deceit and
an enemy of righteousness. Elymus did not ultimately oppose Paul
and Barnabas. He opposed the proclamation of the gospel, and this
was Satan's primary goal—to silence the message of Christ.

Paul said, "Will you ever stop trying to bend the path the Lord
has made straight? Look, the Lord's hand is against you, and he will
darken your world as you have sought to darken others'."

As Paul was speaking, Elymus went blind—an ironic problem
for someone who made his living on the ability to see the future.
Elymus reached out, begging for someone to come take his hand to
lead him away from Paul.

When the proconsul saw the Holy Spirit at work, he believed the
gospel. As he listened to the apostles, he was astonished at the
teachings of the Lord. His conversion greatly encouraged those who
were with Paul. Despite the opposition along the way, the proconsul
of Cyprus came to believe in Christ.

Paul, Barnabas, John Mark, and the others left Cyprus and sailed
north to Perga in Pamphylia. There John Mark pulled his cousin
Barnabas aside and told him he was leaving the party to head home

to Jerusalem. Barnabas loved his cousin and encouraged him. But John Mark's decision bothered Paul. It felt like desertion.

The mission to preach Christ throughout the Roman Empire was dangerous work. James's death and Peter's imprisonment were proof of that. And the mountains of Tarsus the missionaries planned to cross were known to be perilous to honest travelers. Leaving the confines of home to venture into the Gentile world had taken a toll on John Mark's heart. Now he was in a far country, dangerous and strange, and he'd had enough.

Much to Paul's frustration, John Mark left the group in Perga. He went back to Jerusalem as Paul's group prepared to leave for Pisidian Antioch. Their relationship wasn't broken, but it was strained. Barnabas watched in sorrow as his cousin left, then he gathered his things and set them with Paul's, and together they pressed on.

When Paul and Barnabas arrived in Pisidian Antioch, in the southern part of the region of Galatia, they went to the synagogue on the Sabbath. Whenever Paul went to a synagogue, he wore the traditional dress of a rabbi. During the reading of the law, some of the rulers of the synagogue noticed Paul's clothes and sent an attendant to ask if the traveling teacher had a message of encouragement for the people.

Paul stood and motioned for the congregation to listen to him. Then, following a pattern very similar to the message Stephen had given just before his death, Paul delivered a sermon that traced the historical roots of the Jewish people all the way up to the death and resurrection of Jesus Christ. He outlined how Old Covenant history was about a promise fulfilled in Christ. He spoke of how the Jews in Jerusalem had not recognized or accepted Jesus, though Christ was the fulfillment of specific prophecies in the law of God.

Paul concluded his message with an appeal for the people to respond, warning them not to dismiss the gospel message but to weigh it carefully. Many put their faith in Jesus then and there, but there were also many who needed more time. This was all very new. Many were taking Paul's words to heart—weighing this message he proclaimed—but some wanted to hear more. So a group of them asked Paul and Barnabas to come back in a week to tell them more about Jesus.

The apostles were discovering that this was how evangelism often worked. When they proclaimed Christ, people would sometimes take weeks, months, or even years to consider what had been said. This was consistent with the nature of the message Paul and his companions proclaimed. If the gospel of Jesus was true, it was an "accept or reject" proposition. If Jesus was the Savior of the world, and the only Savior, then the news of his resurrection was relevant to everyone.

When Paul and Barnabas returned to the synagogue the following week, the whole city gathered to hear them. Many came because Paul and Barnabas were travelers, which made them a precious source of information for the residents of this landlocked city a hundred miles off the coast. Paul and Barnabas had come from Cyprus. They had recently visited Jerusalem. People with loved ones or interests in those places hoped Paul and Barnabas might give them news.

But many came because the gospel Paul delivered was news itself. Those who had heard Paul speak the week before recognized that his message was different from anything they had heard. It was news and thus a matter of curiosity.

When the religious leaders saw the crowds that had gathered, they were filled with jealousy and began to speak against Paul and his companions, rejecting his message. They were offended by the idea that God would not accept them based on their own efforts to make themselves righteous before him. They could not accept the notion that God would accept those who had not made themselves righteous before him. They assumed the law of Moses was given so they might prove themselves worthy of God by their conduct. They did not see that the law of Moses held up a mirror to the darkness in their hearts, revealing that they are all, by nature, lawbreakers.

They were offended that although Paul brought the gospel to the Jews first, it was not an exclusively Jewish gospel. It was the gospel between God and humanity. The idea that God would accept a Gentile straight out of paganism, without converting to Judaism first, was a line too far. And it was a line Paul and Barnabas were becoming increasingly familiar with.

After preaching Christ to the Jews in Pisidian Antioch, Paul took his message to the Gentiles in that city. They were glad to hear the gospel, and many took to heart the Word of God, receiving the apostles' teaching as a guide for how they should live and as a standard that should overrule their own desires when the two were in conflict.

The Gentile coverts in Antioch understood that to accept Christ meant more than simply to believe in him. To receive him as Lord over everything was to receive his call to go and make disciples— and to do so out of deep gladness for hearing the Word of the Lord. That is just what these Gentile converts did. As a result, the Word of the Lord spread throughout Galatia.

16

THERE AND BACK AGAIN

Acts 14:1-28

LEAVING ANTIOCH, PAUL, BARNABAS, and their group traveled southwest along the plateau between Tarsus and the Sultan Mountains to the old city of Iconium. Iconium was one of Galatia's centers of farming and commerce.

When they arrived, they followed their regular pattern—preaching in the synagogue first, then taking the gospel to the Gentiles. They spoke in such a way that a great number of Jews and Gentiles believed. But another pattern in their work was forming as well—many of those who rejected Christ strongly opposed Paul and Barnabas, stirring up the people to lash out against the apostles, hoping to poison the message of the gospel. The apostles had found this sort of opposition in Jerusalem, in Paphos, and also in Pisidian Antioch. This cycle of vitriol yielded yet another pattern—the manner in which Paul and Barnabas responded.

Though many react to opposition by trying to leave the situation, Paul planted his feet and stayed in the fight. When hostility arose in Iconium, Paul told those with him that they should stay and continue proclaiming Christ even more boldly. They pushed back, stood up, and contended for the truth of the gospel, remaining there for some time. The Lord was with them, granting them the ability to perform signs and wonders so the people would see and believe.

The apostles did not attempt to find middle ground with those opposing their teaching. Rather, they taught the whole gospel. Many had come to faith, and these new converts needed Paul, Barnabas, and the others to disciple them in the faith.

As it often goes with conflict, when Paul and Barnabas pushed back against those who spoke against them, the opposition got organized. The unbelieving Jews and Gentiles in Iconium plotted to stone Paul and his friends to death. When Paul and Barnabas learned of this, they fled the city and made their way to Lystra and Derbe—cities in the region of Lycaonia in Galatia—and continued preaching Christ there.

Paul's tenacity to continue preaching demonstrated that he did not flee Iconium because he was wilting under the opposition. He fled so they could continue to do the very thing they were being opposed for—preaching Christ and him crucified. It was a strategic, gospel-furthering move to depart.

Lystra was a city dominated by the worship of the Greek god Zeus. Paul gathered a crowd of Gentiles and began to teach them about the resurrected Christ and his power to restore the sick and broken. There was a man listening who had been paralyzed since birth. Recognizing a glimmer of faith in the man, Paul looked at him and said, "Stand up." A rush of sensation filled the man's legs, and he sprang up and began walking. The man was overcome with joy. The people did not know what to make of what they had just seen, so they fell back on their Greek religion and said, "The gods have visited us today!"

The crowds began calling Barnabas "Zeus" and Paul "Hermes" in their native tongue and began to worship at the feet of the apostles. Paul and Barnabas did not understand what was happening at first. Local legend was that Zeus and Hermes had visited the town once before, but no one recognized them. These people did not want to repeat that mistake, so the priest of Zeus brought oxen and garlands to the city gate to offer sacrifices to Paul and Barnabas, thinking they were these gods.

This was a new sort of opposition to the gospel. Though Paul and Barnabas had been in many situations where people wanted to harm them because of their message, they had not yet been in a position where people wanted to worship them for it. Pride lurks in the heart, and for men who had more than a dozen miraculous healings under their belts, there was a temptation to take personal credit for the work of God.

Fear gripped Paul and Barnabas as soon as they understood what was happening. They rushed out among the people, tearing their garments and pleading for them to stop. Paul cried out, "Don't do this! Don't worship us. We are men like you. Turn from this vanity and worship the living God who created the heavens and earth and all that is in them."

This was not the response the people wanted. They favored their own narrative—that Paul and Barnabas were the gods their city had revered but not seen in all these years. They wanted to worship the apostles, even as Paul begged them not to, because they feared upsetting the gods.

Paul used the misunderstanding as an occasion to preach Christ with even more clarity to this most captive audience. Often misunderstanding opens the door to even greater clarity. Paul's message to these Gentiles was different from what he preached to Jewish audiences. To the Jews, he usually began with references to their history and God's covenant. But to this crowd of pagans, he went back even further—before Abraham all the way to creation itself. All men were united in their beginnings. The living God, Paul said, covered the world with evidence of his presence and blessed his creation with the rains that nourished the crops that sustained their lives. This was the God they should worship. This was the only true God.

The look of adoration began to fade from the crowd as Paul's words took root. The days passed, and Paul and Barnabas saw more and more people place their faith in Jesus. But Paul noticed that many in Lystra still wished they could offer sacrifices to his group.

Before long trouble caught up with Paul and Barnabas in Lystra. A group of Jews from Antioch and Iconium came looking for them. These were the leaders who had incited the people of those cities to drive Paul and Barnabas out during their earlier visits. Their disdain for the ministry of these Christians was as strong as Paul's had ever been before his conversion. The Jews from Iconium and Antioch were now engaged in their own form of proselytizing—preaching against the gospel of Christ and taking their message on the road.

They succeeded in turning the people of Lystra against them. Under the persuasion of the Jewish leaders, the people of Lystra didn't just reject the Christians; they became so agitated that they seized Paul and took him to a courtyard where they stoned him until they thought he was dead. Then they dragged his body outside of the city gate.

People are fickle. That the residents of Lystra could regard Paul as a god one day and try to stone him to death the next was not without precedent. The final week of Jesus' earthly ministry began with him riding triumphant into Jerusalem as the people laid palms at his feet. As he rode by, the people called him the one who came in the name of the Lord. But only a few days later people from that same city demanded his crucifixion.

After the people of Lystra stoned Paul and left him for dead, they cast his body in the dump, assuming they were rid of him. But they were not, and there was only one reason for this: God was not done with Paul. It wasn't Paul's time to die. As it happened with Peter in Jerusalem's Antonia Fortress, when the Lord intends for his servant to live, his servant lives. He is immortal until the Lord decrees otherwise.

Not only did Paul survive, when he awoke he went back into the city. These were not the actions of a halfhearted man but of one singularly devoted to Christ's call. He joined up with Barnabas and his companions and together they headed west for Derbe and preached Christ there. As had happened in every other place they visited, many in Derbe put their faith in Jesus, though others rejected him.

After spending some time in Derbe, Paul and Barnabas decided to head home, retracing their steps by going back through Lystra, Iconium, Pisidian Antioch, and Perga on the way.

For Paul, return trips to these cities were as crucial as his initial visits. Paul's company stopped by all the churches they had helped establish. Paul would follow this pattern of returning to the churches he'd planted throughout his ministry life—visiting when he could, sending letters when he couldn't.

In each town Paul and his companions encouraged the young converts to continue in the faith and not revert back to Judaism or paganism. They talked about the coming trials they would face as new Christians, offering realistic warnings about the difficulty that likely lay ahead for them. They nurtured these congregations and built on the foundation the Lord had set by appointing elders to shepherd those churches—men of wisdom and humility who were full of the Holy Spirit. The Lord did not intend for his people to be a bunch of private converts living independently of one another. He meant for them to be one body, a people who relied on and looked out for one another.

All of this the missionaries did through prayer and fasting as they made their way back to their home church—their sending church in Syrian Antioch. When they finally arrived, they gathered the believers and told them all that the Lord had done in them and through them. They also talked about the trials they had faced, but this was not their focus. They concentrated not on what they had endured but on what God had done among the Gentiles. They had seen the hand of God at work. The Lord was opening wide the door of faith to the Gentile world. What was happening was revolutionary.

The church in Antioch had leaders who were Gentile converts, and they had a large ministry to Gentiles in that city. News that the gospel had spread throughout Galatia was tremendously encouraging to them. They were not alone. God was doing among the nations what he had begun with them, and he had used their congregation to send Paul and Barnabas, whose ministry was now becoming global.

Jesus' Great Commission to preach the gospel to every tribe, tongue, and nation was being fulfilled through them. It was a humble honor to be part of that work—for the church and for Paul and Barnabas, whom the church had commissioned and sent. They had gone out through the major strategic cities in Galatia by the help and power of the Holy Spirit and had, at least in part, fulfilled the task to which they had been called.

As much as the Lord had accomplished through Paul, though, he could not shake the feeling that he was only just getting started.

THE JERUSALEM
COUNCIL

Acts 15:1-35

*T*HE CHURCH IN ANTIOCH WAS GLAD to have Paul, Barnabas, and the others home safe. Paul's companions soon fell into the rhythms of life in their local church—growing in their faith, carrying each other's burdens, and enjoying one another's friendship. The church continued to grow there, and their influence reached into the nearby villages. The gospel of Christ spread in part simply because the church existed. They were a topic of conversation and a fascination to many who heard about their ethnic diversity, their unity and joy, the miracles attributed to their leaders, and the harrowing journey to Galatia from which Paul's group had just returned.

As the gospel message spread out from the church in Antioch, the influence of the church in Jerusalem made its way to them. The two increasing circles were bound to eventually touch. In Antioch, many of the believers were Gentiles. But in Jerusalem and the nearby regions, Jewish culture shaped much of the new and growing Christian community. Men of Jewish origin had established the church, and a great many of those who first put their faith in Jesus, thousands upon thousands, were either Jews or God-fearing Gentiles who had grown up worshiping as the Jews did. So Jewish culture was part of the early Christian expression in and around Jerusalem and Judea.

As a result, it could be difficult for people to discern what parts of their Jewish faith were essential components of Christianity and what parts had either been nullified or fulfilled. Not surprisingly, then, many people struggled with the place of circumcision in the life of a Christian. Some doubted that it should be as prominent in Christianity as it was in Judaism, but many were adamant that it was vital. For them, the thought that circumcision was no longer necessary was unimaginable.

The idea that to convert to Christ a Gentile must also convert to Judaism did not initially come out of a desire to harm the church. It was born from a misunderstanding. Jewish people grew up knowing that to be Jewish was to be circumcised. So if Jesus Christ was the fulfillment of the Jewish law and prophecies as the apostles proclaimed he was, it only made sense that Christians should take the sign that identified them as God's people—circumcision. Until the spread of the gospel to the Gentiles, how circumcision related to Christianity hadn't been much of an issue—Jewish converts were already circumcised. But since circumcision played such an integral role in the identity of God's people, many naturally assumed that Gentile converts to Christ should become like Jews.

Some men from Jerusalem came to the church in Antioch. Paul and the others welcomed them and asked them for a report of all that the Lord had been doing in the Holy City. Paul and Barnabas told them how the gospel was spreading throughout regions like Galatia and how many Gentiles—pagans with no connection to Judaism—were putting their faith in Christ. Some of the men from Jerusalem pressed Paul for more information. Who would teach them the law of Moses? How would they observe the holidays? Were they willing to be circumcised?

Paul said, "We didn't circumcise them. Christians don't need to be circumcised."

The believers in Antioch could feel the tension rise as soon as Paul said this. The men from Jerusalem thought Paul had been careless. They said, "Unless a man is circumcised, according to the custom of Moses, he cannot be saved."

Paul and Barnabas both jumped into the debate, insisting that a person is saved by grace through faith in Christ alone and not by any act of the flesh. The men from Jerusalem insisted that there was sanctity in the ancient traditions and that they must be honored if God was to be pleased.

When the two groups came to a theological impasse, the leaders of the church in Antioch decided the best course of action was to send a delegate from their church—Paul, Barnabas, and some others—to Jerusalem to confer with the apostles there.

As the two groups traveled south together through Phoenicia and Samaria to Jerusalem, Paul and Barnabas told believers in the towns they passed through about the Gentile conversions they had seen. These stories were like medicine to those who heard them—little doses of joy, hope, and courage.

When they arrived in Jerusalem, the apostles there and the elders in the church welcomed them. The council that gathered included Simon Peter, Paul, Barnabas, James the brother of Jesus, John,

Andrew, and several of the other original twelve disciples. This issue concerning the relationship between circumcision and salvation was important to them all. They knew that getting this right was vital to the survival of the growing church.

Paul and Barnabas told them all that the Lord had done in Cyprus, Perga, Pisidian Antioch, Iconium, and Lystra. They spoke of the opposition they faced, but their focus was on how many Gentiles had come to believe in Jesus and how the Holy Spirit had come on them as he had on the Jews who first believed.

Some members of the Pharisee party spoke up: "This is good to hear, but we have to ask: How can a person keep the law of Moses without being circumcised? They can't."

The apostles and elders gathered to discuss the matter. Their discussion turned into a lengthy debate. This was a tough question for many former Jews. After listening and weighing his colleagues' words, Peter spoke. He said that imposing circumcision would be wrong. From his perspective, this was less about circumcision itself than how God gave the Holy Spirit to the Gentiles at Cornelius's home after he preached there.

Peter said, "I remember how the Lord worked in that situation with Cornelius. God made no distinction between us and them. He cleansed their hearts by faith. I am a witness to that. He saved the Gentiles there without requiring circumcision. And if God made no distinction, why should we?"

Paul and Barnabas both rose and told the council more of how God had worked among the Gentiles in Asia Minor. What God was doing in the Gentile world was already underway, and the lack of circumcision had not proven to be an obstacle. If God was already calling Gentiles to himself, who were they to overrule God's process and add a ceremonial requirement to grace through faith in Christ alone?

When they finished speaking, James, the brother of Jesus, said, "Listen, our brother Simon Peter has himself testified here and now of how he has seen the Lord work among the Gentiles. He witnessed genuine conversions, and this aligns with what Scripture tells us."

James then appealed to the writings of the old prophet Amos, who said that God would rebuild his people from a remnant that would include "all the Gentiles who are called by my name." The Lord had made these things known from of old. What God was doing among the Gentiles was not a new idea. It was an ancient promise.

For these men who had cast out demons and performed miraculous healings, their approach to answering the question of circumcision might have seemed pedestrian to an outsider who knew them by reputation only. They received no angelic visit to deliver a supernatural word from the Lord. But God was not silent. He had spoken to their question hundreds of years earlier through the prophet Amos. Their responsibility was to discern the existing Word that was timeless, authoritative, and true.

So they did. They debated, read, prayed, and listened. When they had heard from everyone, James said, "It is my judgment that we should not require Gentiles to be circumcised when they believe in Jesus. They do not need to put on Judaism. But they will need to put off much of what is common among the pagans. Let's write a letter freeing them from the burden of circumcision but urging them toward personal holiness."

The Jerusalem Council agreed with James. They drafted their response in a letter and sent both Paul and Peter, along with several others from Jerusalem, back to Antioch to deliver the news. In that group was a man named Silas, a leader in the Jerusalem church who was a gifted speaker. Silas looked forward to meeting these believers in Antioch so he could encourage them and be cheered by them. As the group was leaving, the apostles in Jerusalem asked Paul to remember the poor in Jerusalem as he traveled. They needed the church at large to help care for them during their famine years. Paul promised to remember them and determined that he would take up a collection for them in every church he visited.

In the letter from the Jerusalem Council, the apostles ruled that the Gentiles were free from the burden of circumcision. Not surprisingly, the uncircumcised Gentile converts in Antioch received the apostles' letter with great gladness, as did the entire community.

Along with the ruling on circumcision came the call to take responsibility for any conduct that might cause a brother or sister in Christ to stumble. The council gave the Gentiles two specific admonitions—to abstain from eating meat sacrificed to idols and to abstain from sexual immorality. The second admonition was easy to understand. But the first, to abstain from eating meat sacrificed to idols, was given for the sake of the Jewish conscience. There were Jews in every city. Eating meat sacrificed to idols could easily defile the consciences of those who grew up knowing they were to have nothing to do with false gods. So the council told them all to abstain.

Jews and Gentiles would be saved in the same way—not by law keeping, circumcision, or anything else, but by grace alone. Gentile Christians were not required to embrace the customs of the Jews, but they were responsible to care about the consciences of their Jewish brothers and sisters and to live accordingly. And Jewish Christians were not required to abandon the traditions of their faith, but they were responsible to respect the fact that their Gentile brothers and sisters would see the world differently. Both groups were to see this call to humility as a strength and a sign that God's love included them even as it reached beyond them.

The believers in Antioch celebrated this report, but old habits die hard. Peter and his delegate from Jerusalem stayed in Antioch for a while, learning more about how the Lord was working. The church in Antioch was an important study for the apostles because it was largely made up of Greeks who had come to believe in Jesus Christ. During Peter's time in Antioch, some Jewish converts from the Jerusalem church came for a visit. These men insisted on keeping the Jewish ceremonial diet, which forbade sharing a table with anyone who was not ceremonially clean. Peter, a Jew himself, felt the pressure to honor their conviction, and he stopped eating his meals with Gentile Christians.

When Peter withdrew from the Gentiles, Barnabas followed his lead. When Paul saw what was happening, he publicly rebuked Peter. He said, "You are a Jew but you live like a Gentile. Works of the law have no power. You know this. You live in the freedom of this. So why are you now forcing Gentiles to live like Jews through your hypocrisy? Why are you rebuilding what the gospel has torn down?"

Paul's rebuke cut Peter to the heart. He knew he had sinned and repented of it. The gospel itself was at stake. There was no Jew or Greek in Christ. To show favoritism to the Jews could be born only of the idea that God favored the Jews, undermining the entire saving work of Christ. Peter's behavior was born of hypocrisy, not conviction. Peter did not believe God favored the Jews over the Gentiles. His behavior came from an insincere fear of man. It wasn't that Peter had a different opinion than Paul. It was that he was actively betraying his own conviction. His actions had consequences; other people, including Barnabas, followed him. Peter was wrong and he knew it.

Paul and Barnabas had a history on this matter, and Peter saw that it hurt Paul to see Barnabas yield ground the two of them had suffered so much to gain. Barnabas and Paul had seen the gospel perverted before, and as a unified front they had stood to uphold the truth. But now his dear friend in ministry—who had labored beside him, fought for the purity of the gospel, stood in opposition to false teachers, and summoned the Jerusalem Council to get a definitive answer on whether there was any distinction between Jew and Gentile in Christ—now joined Peter in his hypocrisy. Barnabas stood with Peter in the wrong, and Peter knew Paul knew Barnabas knew it was wrong.

This was not the first time Peter had been a walking contradiction, and it wouldn't be the last. He received Paul's rebuke more as a lifeline than as a hammer blow. Paul applied truth to Peter's brokenness like a balm when he said, "We know a person is not justified by works of the law but through faith in Jesus Christ. This is why we have believed in Christ, so that we might be justified by faith in him and not by works of the law. No one has ever been or ever will be justified by works of the law. I have been crucified with Christ. It is no longer I who live. Christ lives in me, and this life we now live in the flesh we live by faith in the Son of God who loved us and gave himself for us."

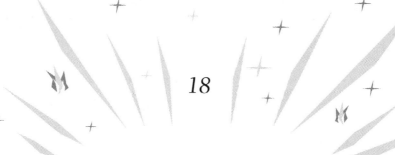

18

COME OVER
AND HELP US

Acts 15:36–16:15

*P*AUL, *B*ARNABAS, *AND THE BELIEVERS* in Antioch were energized by the apostles' conclusion on the matter of whether circumcision was required for salvation. The answer was that Christ alone saved. Circumcision was not a requirement for a person's entry into the family of God. When Paul and Barnabas got this news, they brought it back to their home church, where it was received with great joy.

Thinking of the other believers spread throughout Galatia who were wrestling with the same questions of law and grace, Paul wrote a letter to be circulated among the churches there. In it he discussed how there was no other gospel but the saving work of Christ on their behalf. No rituals or old traditions would bring them close to God. Only Christ himself could do that. Their only justification before God came through Jesus, who made those who believed in him children of God—heirs with Christ. They were a people set free to run the race set before them with the confidence of knowing they lived now by the power of the Spirit of God. He urged them to live in the humility and confidence of the finished work of Christ and to look for their justification before God in no other place.

But as Paul thought about the report from the Jerusalem Council and how difficult it would likely be for Gentile converts in other cities to believe they belonged in full measure to the body of Christ, Paul planned to return to them in person. It was not enough for him to bring this report simply to his home church. He needed to take it far and wide so the church would know, as it continued to grow, that salvation was a work of God's grace through faith in Christ alone. Paul turned his thinking to a second journey to deliver this message from the Jerusalem Council, lest anyone try to impose on any Christian the burden of circumcision. On this journey he would return to the cities in Galatia and Phrygia he had visited earlier, and then he would take the gospel beyond them, as far as he could.

While the first missionary journey had begun with a long season of prayer and fasting and a special commissioning of Paul and Barnabas by the elders of the church in Antioch, the second happened much more expeditiously. There was no need for special commissioning because the call to take the gospel to the Gentiles was a standing call. This was the work for which Paul and Barnabas had been set apart. They began to plan.

As they prepared to leave, Barnabas and Paul discussed who should go with them. Barnabas told Paul that John Mark wanted to join them again. But when John Mark had left them in the middle of the previous missionary journey, Paul had regarded it as desertion. Paul also believed that this journey would be harder than the first. They would, after all, return to the same cities they'd previously been thrown out of—even stoned in. Lives were at stake here. So he told Barnabas he didn't want John Mark to come along. How could Barnabas tell his own cousin he couldn't come? This wasn't in Barnabas's nature. As his name, the Son of Encouragement, suggested, Barnabas was disposed to believe the best of people. He believed so strongly that John Mark should come with them that it led to a sharp disagreement between him and Paul. Seeing he could not persuade Paul, Barnabas took a stand for his cousin and opted to stay behind with him rather than travel on.

Barnabas, the protégé of Peter and the mentor of Paul, was a man of daring faith and humble leadership, but he was also weak, and his weakness sometimes carried the day. Barnabas was confident in God's ability to work in dire circumstances. He trusted that God's plan to redeem his people didn't hinge on his own participation. Barnabas's decision to stand with his cousin was not a thing to be pitied but admired. His strength was his weakness. Still, his loyalty to John Mark carried with it this consequence: Silas would go in his place.

Paul was caught in the classic struggle over choosing which to put first—relationships or the work at hand. Paul and Barnabas were close allies, but Paul's mission was to the Gentiles throughout Rome. He operated on the principle that the call to do the work of Christ was prime. Anything that jeopardized that mission was second to the mission itself.

So Paul parted with Barnabas over John Mark and took Silas, who had joined them from the church in Jerusalem. Barnabas set sail for his hometown of Cyprus, where he continued to minister in the name of Christ among his countrymen. John Mark continued to proclaim Christ as well. But these three men would never travel together again.

Paul and Silas's route essentially traced Paul's first journey in reverse. They went to Tarsus first, then to Derbe and Lystra, where Paul had previously been stoned and left for dead. Then they went to Iconium and Antioch, where those who stoned Paul had come from. With the exception of Derbe, Paul and Barnabas had been thrown out of all these cities. But they returned anyway to encourage and strengthen the churches that had formed as the result of their first visit.

During Paul's first visit to Lystra, a young man named Timothy had come to believe in Christ, and now Timothy was growing in his reputation as a man of God. Paul saw great potential in the young man and wanted to bring him on the rest of the journey.

But it wasn't just Timothy's personality that Paul valued. It was his pedigree too. Timothy was half Jewish, half Greek. Paul's ministry was to both Jews and Greeks throughout Rome. Timothy could represent Christ to both audiences—but there was one problem. Timothy wasn't circumcised. Even though Paul adamantly opposed the need for Christians to be circumcised, he required Timothy to be circumcised because he wanted Timothy to have credibility with the Jewish people they would meet in the cities they would visit.

Was this hypocrisy? For Paul this was more consistency than hypocrisy. He had separated from Barnabas because he wanted nothing to stand in the way of bringing the gospel to Rome. For this same reason he had Timothy circumcised. He wanted Timothy to have a voice among the Jews. And to the Jewish mind, an uncircumcised half-Jew was essentially a full Gentile.

Paul's theology of circumcision was clear. He had already fought to make believers understand that circumcision was unnecessary for acceptance with God. This was the very message he planned to deliver to the Jews he met. But he also knew that circumcision was still advisable for acceptance with some people. The purpose of this missionary journey was not to appease Christian Jews but rather to gain an audience with unbelieving Jews. So even though Paul was an iron pillar when it came to the essentials, he was a flexible reed in the non-essentials—bending to be all things to all people. He made up his mind not to put any stumbling block in his brother's way. To do this among the Jews, he had Timothy circumcised.

Paul, Silas, and Timothy traveled west to Pisidian Antioch. After spending a little time there, they prepared to continue west through the Roman province of Asia. But the Holy Spirit forbade Paul from entering that province, so they set their sights north to the region of Bithynia. The Spirit did not allow them to go there either. The only possible route that remained for them was the corridor to Mysia on the edge of the Aegean Sea. This road ran right between Asia and Bithynia and led to the coastal city of Troas.

When Paul, Silas, Timothy, and those who were with them came to Troas, a physician named Luke, who had become a follower of Jesus, joined with them. Luke was a doctor, as well as a historian and writer. Ever since he had put his faith in Jesus, Luke had had an insatiable appetite to learn, understand, and document the life, death, and resurrection of Jesus of Nazareth. And he was equally interested in the life and growth of the early Christian church.

Though no one could say at the time why God forbade Paul to enter Asia or Bithynia, the purpose would soon become clear. While in Troas, Paul had a vision of a man from Macedonia pleading, "Come over and help us!" Paul had never seen the man before, but he told his companions about the vision. The man asked for help but didn't specify what kind of help he needed. What else did Paul have to give? His group concluded this meant God was calling them to bring the gospel to Macedonia near Greece, which would be the first time these missionaries set foot in Europe proper.

Paul, Silas, Timothy, Luke, and the others set sail for Macedonia, stopping on the island of Samothrace—a breathtaking rocky island with five-thousand-foot peaks towering above. From there they had their choice of Macedonian ports. They chose Neapolis because it was only a ten-mile walk from there to Philippi, a leading city in Macedonia and a Roman colony. Philippi seemed a good place to begin.

In Philippi, on the Sabbath, Paul sought a hearing with the Jews first, as was his custom. There were some followers of Judaism there but not enough to establish a synagogue, which required at least ten men to form a quorum. With no synagogue, the Jews in Philippi gathered at a place outside the city. They were mostly women. One of the women who gathered with them was a widow named Lydia, a God-fearing Gentile.

Lydia was textile merchant from Thyatira, a town known for its production of purple dye. As Paul preached the gospel to Lydia and the others gathered by the river just outside of Philippi, the Lord opened her heart to pay attention to what Paul was saying. It was not Paul's eloquence that brought Lydia to faith. It was God, who gave her ears to hear. Conversion never comes just through hearing but in power and in the Holy Spirit, who brings full conviction.

Lydia was the first known convert to Christ in all of Europe. Her house became the center of the church in Philippi, which would become a major hub of encouragement for Paul in his mission to Europe.

Lydia sealed her profession of faith with baptism, and her household was baptized with her. Lydia had a home there and acted as its head. In those days a household consisted of everyone who lived under the same roof—children, parents, and servants. After Lydia's household was baptized, she urged Paul and the others to stay with her, which they did.

19

THE PHILIPPIAN
PRECEDENT

Acts 16:16-40

*I*T WAS MORNING IN PHILIPPI. Paul and Silas stood in a prison cell. They had been beaten the night before. They were bruised, sore, and tired. The door to the cell door stood open, and the jailer was telling them they were now free to go. But with gates open and freedom offered, Paul refused to leave. He wanted some satisfaction first. He wanted an apology.

Though Paul had been brought to that jail as a criminal, he refused to leave on principle. Paul knew the Lord worked in mysterious ways. There was no situation over which God did not rule, so Paul read his own circumstances and decided that the injustice that had been done to him the day before was an opportunity for him to complicate things for those who wanted to leverage political power to persecute Christians—and also to protect missionaries who would come after him.

The day before, as Paul, Silas, Timothy, and the others in their party were going to the place of prayer in Philippi, they had passed by a slave girl who was exploited by her owners for profit. She worked as a fortune-teller who would fall into a trancelike, manic state—proclaiming whatever she saw in her mind about the futures of those who paid her.

The girl had been following Paul around for days, announcing to everyone that he was a servant of the Most High God who was proclaiming the way of salvation. Though no one knew how, she had alighted on the truth. Paul tried to ignore her because he didn't want to stir up trouble in that town. But soon his patience wore thin. The girl's behavior called to mind the story Peter had told Paul about a demon-possessed man who followed Jesus around, calling him the Holy One of God. Jesus expelled that demon, so Paul decided he would follow Jesus' lead by rebuking the evil spirit in this girl.

The reason Paul tried to delay speaking to the slave girl was that situations like these got him and his friends into trouble, which often meant they had to move on. Paul knew that when he cast out the demon the slave girl would lose her ability to tell fortunes, which would cost her owners income. No one in the history of commerce has taken kindly to a loss of income. But he couldn't let her go on like this either. Eventually he looked at the girl and said, "In the name of Jesus, I command you to come out of her." Immediately the girl's countenance changed, and what had possessed her was now gone.

When the girl's slave owners discovered what had happened, they went to the authorities to bring charges against Paul and Silas. Knowing that a story about lost income wouldn't achieve much of a result in court, they brought a different charge—one they hoped would get better results. The girl's slave owners accused Paul and

Silas of being Jews who were throwing the city into an uproar by advocating customs that were unlawful for Romans. This was a lie, but Philippi was settled by retired Roman soldiers who were very proud of their citizenship. The charge that Paul and his friends were using their Judaism to disrupt the Roman way of life carried weight with the magistrates. Without a trial, the magistrates ordered their soldiers to seize Paul and Silas, beat them with rods, cast them into prison, and fasten their feet in stocks like criminals.

The jailer knew his new charges were unusual prisoners. Paul and Silas didn't complain, strategize, or protest their unjust treatment. Instead, they prayed and sang hymns to God. The other prisoners listened with fascination. Though this time in prison could have led to their execution, Paul and Silas behaved as men who had the hope of eternal life—a hope that informs how a person handles hardship.

While they were singing, a sudden earthquake shook the place, opening the cells and loosing the stocks that bound these men. The jailer, who had been sleeping, awoke with the world crashing down on him.

"No, no, no," he cried as he ran to find the cell doors all standing open. Seeing this, he concluded the prisoners were long gone. Being a Roman soldier, he knew the penalty for permitting a prisoner to escape was death, so he prepared to take that penalty on himself by falling on his sword.

The jailer drew his sword and studied the tip a moment—the steel that would run him through. Then he lowered the point to the place just below his lower rib. As he was about to lean into his death, he heard Paul call out to him.

"Jailer, stop! Don't harm yourself. We're all still here."

The jailer dropped his sword and came trembling into the cell row. When he saw that none of his prisoners had escaped, he fell to his knees and wept.

The moment was hard for the jailer to describe. Though he held the highest civil authority in the room, he was certain he was also the most doomed man there. But in Paul's words he heard the voice of his salvation. If the prisoners had not fled, they had saved his life. In an ironic twist, the prisoners who had been singing praise to God all night held the key to the jailer's freedom.

The jailer knew the charges that had been brought against Paul. He also knew about the transformation that had happened to the slave girl who had said Paul was proclaiming the way of salvation. The rumor around town was that Paul and Silas had come in the power of the Most High God. The jailer believed he was seeing this power firsthand when he witnessed how even in their darkest night, Paul and Silas praised God as though he alone was their salvation. Out of gratitude for their presence and fear of the power in which they came, the jailer asked what he had to do to be saved into eternal life in the presence of this holy, Most High God.

Paul said, "Believe in the Lord Jesus Christ, and you will be saved—you and your entire household."

The jailer gathered his family and all who were in his house, and they listened as Paul and Silas told them about the risen Christ. As they spoke, the jailer noticed their wounds from the previous night's beating. He sent for a bowl and a fresh cloth, and he cleansed their wounds as they told him about the cleansing waters of baptism.

When Paul and Silas finished telling them about Christ, the jailer believed and was baptized, along with the rest of his family. Then he brought Paul and Silas up into his house above the jail and gave them some food. The jailer was filled with joy over his newfound faith, and his family rejoiced with him. The conversation, food, and friendship these people shared that night led to the jailer's conversion and also forged a lasting bond of friendship between them all. Paul told the jailer about Lydia and the church, and the jailer and his family soon became a part of the fellowship of Christians in Philippi.

After spending a few hours at the jailer's house, Paul and Silas returned to the prison before dawn. That morning the jailer received orders from the magistrates to release Paul and Silas. The magistrates figured the beatings the Christians had taken and their night in the stocks would keep them from causing any more trouble in Philippi. When the jailer delivered the news, he smiled and said, "Go in peace, my brothers."

Paul said, "We cannot do that. Listen, the magistrates beat us publicly without any trial. We were uncondemned men—Roman citizens, in fact. How they treated us is against Roman law. Do they imagine they can throw us into prison so publicly, then throw us out in secret? Tell the magistrates to come and lead us out themselves. We'll wait."

The magistrates knew the initial accusations brought against Paul were thin, and they had reacted impulsively against these men accused of acting against their homeland. In their minds what they did was for the glory of Rome and for the education of any who would disrespect her. But they failed to consider one crucial detail. What if these men were in fact Roman citizens themselves? Roman citizens were exempt from any kind of formal public beating or imprisonment without a fair trial.

In the name of Rome's nobility and glory, the magistrates had behaved in a decidedly un-Roman manner by violating the honor of the citizenship they thought they were defending. All they wanted now was for Paul and Silas to go away—thus washing their hands of this mess before news of what they had done reached a higher court.

But Paul refused to cooperate. Instead he and Silas took their seats in their cells. They would not budge until they had their apology. When the magistrates heard this, they realized that in their bravado they had caught a tiger by the tail. Letting Paul go would not be nearly as easy as apprehending him.

Paul insisted on receiving the best treatment the law afforded because he knew the Lord was building his church in Philippi. He also knew Christians everywhere were facing persecution. The magistrates' failure to follow Roman law was an opportunity to bring some protection to this church. How the magistrates treated Paul and Silas would set a precedent for how other Christians would be treated in Philippi. Paul recognized he had an opportunity to shape what that treatment would look like. He would make officials think twice before persecuting other Christians there.

Paul knew it was not the sovereignty of the magistrates that landed him in jail. It was the sovereignty of God. He was not a victim. He was a servant of the Lord who ruled over every moment. This is why when the gates swung open and the magistrates declared the matter settled, Paul disagreed. This was not their moment. It was God's. And what happened to Paul in Philippi had far less to do with his own safety than protecting other Christians in the future.

The magistrates came and apologized to Paul and Silas and asked them to please leave the city. Paul had little use for spite, so he agreed to the magistrates' request and went to Lydia's house to say goodbye. When the believers gathered, Paul told them what had happened. After they encouraged one another, Paul and Silas, along with Timothy, Luke, and the others in their party, set off for Thessalonica.

20

CONCERNING THE UNKNOWN GOD

Acts 17:1-34

*F*OLLOWING THE GREAT ROMAN HIGHWAY, the Via Egnatia—a
seven-hundred-mile road that stretched from the Black Sea to
the Adriatic Sea across Asia—Paul and company headed southwest
down to the Macedonian capital of Thessalonica. When they arrived, Paul went to the synagogue and began preaching Christ. For
three weeks Paul returned, reasoning with the Jews from the Scriptures, explaining and proving why it was necessary for Jesus Christ
to suffer and to rise from the dead.

Paul's message was not focused on mere emotion or experience.
The gospel is a message of doctrinal precision. There are things that
are true about Jesus and things that are false. Understanding correct
doctrine mattered to Paul. There was no gospel without it. So he
settled into a routine of regularly teaching the doctrines of Christianity in Thessalonica.

Paul stayed with a Christian in Thessalonica named Jason. During his time there, Paul's preaching was blessed by God. Some received it eagerly. Believers there tried to model their faith after Paul's, and they ended up becoming models themselves to all the believers in the region. The Thessalonian church contributed aid to Paul's collection for the poor in the Jerusalem church and also became interested in supporting the ongoing mission of the church at large.

Many in Thessalonica believed—both Jews and Gentiles, men and women. But many opposed Paul too. Some of the men in the city were jealous of Paul's reception among the Gentiles, so they trumped up the same charged Paul faced in Philippi—that Paul was calling people to bow the knee to a king other than Caesar—and they set out to have him arrested. They gathered up a band of troublemakers and formed a mob in order to set the city in an uproar. The mob invaded Jason's house, seeking to bring Paul and his companions out to face the angry crowd.

Paul wasn't there. Wanting satisfaction, the leaders of the mob arrested Jason and a couple of others instead and accused them of treason for being friends with this Paul, who they said was turning the rest of the world upside down and was about to do so to their community too. It was a strange accusation—a backhanded compliment to the work of Christ in the world. The gospel had gained a reputation for changing people wherever it was proclaimed, and many found that upsetting.

The city authorities made Jason pay a fine and promise he would send Paul and the others on their way the first chance he got. Orders to leave town were usually based on flimsy charges that would be embarrassing to prosecute. No one wanted to deal with the political and social consequence of ruling over a kangaroo court. It was usually easier if the problem just went away. The apostles didn't really want to go through these paces either, so when Jason told them what had happened, they did as they had done in Philippi— they complied and went to Berea during the night to avoid the mob that had as yet been unable to do anything with their fervor.

In Berea, Paul wasted no time going to the synagogue to preach. Again, Jews and Gentiles, men and women believed Paul's message. Curious, the Bereans met daily with Paul. They came at his teaching not with their emotions but with their minds. They received his words eagerly, examining the Scriptures to see whether Paul was teaching truth.

The Bereans wanted to know whether Paul was presenting doctrine or indoctrination. Indoctrination demanded that everything taught be received with uncritical acceptance. Teaching true doctrine, however, meant Paul had to build reasoned arguments on scriptural truths. This process allowed plenty of room for questions. There could be no plucking verses out of context. As Paul built his case, the Bereans searched the Scriptures to see if what he taught held water.

Reasoned arguments and the proclamation of the gospel go hand in hand. The gospel is a reasoned argument, explaining why people are the way they are, why they lack what they lack, what they are meant to be, and how that can be put right in their lives here and now and also in eternity. The Bereans used Paul's message as an occasion to listen, think, ask questions, and find answers.

Soon, the news that Paul and the others were teaching in Berea circled back to Thessalonica. Though Paul and the others faced no substantial opposition from the Bereans, men from the synagogue in Thessalonica traveled to Berea to continue their quest to bring Paul down. They began agitating and stirring up the crowds. It wasn't hard to do. Paul was living like a man who had a king other than Caesar. He talked about Jesus as reigning over a kingdom. He called Jesus a king—his king. Paul even claimed to be a citizen of Christ's kingdom first, before all others.

But Paul did not mean Jesus was going to overthrow Caesar and rule Rome. What Paul meant was even more incredible than that. He meant to say Jesus didn't need Rome to have a kingdom. Rome was the greatest kingdom in the history of the world. But Jesus' kingdom, Paul understood, was even greater—infinitely greater, in fact. Paul considered himself a citizen of that kingdom because he was a child of God through faith in Jesus. Paul was not teaching about a king who would one day rule Rome. He was talking about a king who already ruled over everything, everywhere.

Once this point of doctrine had been reduced to a political threat, tensions rose so much that Paul again had to flee. He made his way down to the famous Greek city of Athens. Silas and Timothy stayed in Berea.

The people escorting Paul took him by sea. Once he arrive in the great city he sent for Silas and Timothy to come join him as soon as possible. While Paul waited for their arrival, he walked the city and was overwhelmed by the wonderful art and architecture. Athens was the intellectual and religious center of Greece, named after the Greek goddess Athena. Athens was a city built on the free exchange of ideas. As was usually the case with cultures like that, it was also a city filled with idols. It was said that it was easier to meet a god or a goddess on the main street of Athens than it was to meet a man. And this was true. This city of ten thousand people was home to thirty thousand idols.

Paul grew up as a Roman citizen, which was heavily influenced by Greek culture, so Athens was a familiar environment. He wasn't shocked to see the idolatry, but he was saddened by it because it reminded him of humanity's hunger for God and the reality of their separation from him.

Paul reached out to the philosophers to tell them about Jesus. The philosophical community, which was Greek, not Jewish, caught bits of his teaching and wanted to hear more. So they brought him out from the Abrahamic setting of the synagogue into the anything-goes setting of the Areopagus—Athens's philosophical hub.

Athenians subscribed to one of the two dominant philosophical schools of thought in Greek culture—Epicureanism and Stoicism. Epicureans believed things happened by chance. The aim of life was pleasure. If something felt good, they should do it. If it didn't, they should avoid it. They believed in gods but not in an afterlife. They believed the simple life was the most pleasurable. Stoics, on the other hand, believed in destiny. They could not change what would happen, but they could control themselves. Their solution to pain was to stand tall, whatever happened, and try to live free from worldly trappings.

As Paul studied the people and their city, he sought to engage them on points they shared in common. He began looking for what he could affirm about their beliefs. This skill required courage because Paul had to be willing to look for elements of truth in the lives of non-Christian people and learn from what he saw without fear that it would topple his faith.

In Paul's opening words in the Areopagus, he affirmed that the Athenians were religious people who had an obvious desire to know and worship God, as evidenced by the volume of idols in their city. They believed God must be greater than man, otherwise they wouldn't worship as they did. And they believed they were meant to interact with God regularly and reverentially. All of this, Paul understood, was in them because God has put in everyone a desire to know him. Even the basest attempt to worship was evidence of being made by God. Paul saw this as common ground.

Paul also affirmed their hunger for knowledge. The Athenians loved to talk about ideas. Paul was saying something new, so they wanted to hear more. For some, this was nothing more than a form of entertainment. For others, it was a sincere pursuit of truth. Others still were in between. Either way, Paul brought them something they prized: knowledge.

In Athens, there was an altar dedicated to an "unknown god." The knowledge Paul brought was the identity of their unknown god. That altar's existence recognized God's presence. The question that had always troubled the Athenians was whether this god minded being unknown. From this question, Paul moved into the content of his gospel message by getting specific. In the gospel of Jesus Christ, the unknown becomes known, the relative becomes absolute. The pluralistic becomes singular. And the knowledge of the one true God demands a response. Paul introduced Christ in such a way that the Athenians had to either accept or reject the information.

Paul built his case on four points. He taught them that God was the creator of everything. God made the world and all that is in it. He did not live in temples built by human hands. He revealed himself. As a garden testifies of a gardener, creation testifies of a Creator. God is the originator of our lives.

God was also the sustainer of everything. God gave all men life and breath and everything else. People served their objects of worship, enshrining them in fancy temples so the world would appreciate their worth. But God did not need humankind to call attention to his glory or to sustain his credibility. He sustained the world, including each person's life and breath.

God also ordained all things. God was intimately involved with his creation. Paul told the Athenians that God determined their lives down to where and when they lived.

Finally, Paul told them that God engages his people so that they might seek him. If God engages his creation, what does it mean for a man to fail to engage him? How lost must a person be to not know the God who created, sustains, and ordains what happens in his creation?

The people were listening, following along until Paul began to talk about Christ being raised from the dead. Greek philosophers often said that when the dust soaked up a dead man's blood there was no resurrection. If there was no life after death, this life had no real meaning. Paul's sermon raised a simple question: Was that true? Were the Greek philosophers correct?

The Greeks were dichotomists. They believed people had a body and a soul. The soul, they said, was the good part of man—the immortal part. The body, on the other hand, was bad. It was meant to perish.

Paul waded into their disbelief concerning the resurrection with a pastor's care. He pleaded with them to believe. He said, "God is not far from any of us. As your own poets have said, 'In him we live and move and have our being.' You are God's offspring. He will judge the world, and our ignorance will not excuse us. Repent and trust in the one who will represent you before your Maker—the one he raised from the dead."

But when Paul began to talk about the bodily resurrection of Christ, his audience not only found this hard to believe, they found it undesirable. In their minds, death would liberate the soul from the body of flesh it had to lug around, and this was seen as a good thing. When Paul appealed to the risen Christ, the room erupted in disbelief and laughter. It was enough of a disruption to end hope of any further orderly presentation.

On the whole, Paul's experience in Athens was discouraging. The gospel seemed to struggle to find fertile soil. But a man named Dionysius, a ranking philosopher in the Areopagus, and Damaris, one of the women present, believed in Christ, along with a few others. Many mocked Paul. But over the din of disbelief, these and a few others pulled Paul aside and said they wanted to hear more.

21

THE ROADS GOOD
FRIENDS WALK

Acts 18:1-23

*L*IFE ON THE MOVE WAS A CONSTANT STRUGGLE. As Paul moved
from city to city through the Roman Empire, each village was
completely new. He didn't know many of the people he encountered
along the way except for a few new friends like Timothy and Titus.
Just as one city began to feel familiar, he would leave or be driven
out to another new place known to him only by its reputation.
Then he would begin again, getting to know the people, the streets,
and the tenor of the place.

Paul had a hard time in Athens. Though he tried to persuade
the philosophers to believe in Jesus, it would be years before a
church would exist there. This entire journey was taking its toll.
So far he had been persecuted, imprisoned, mocked, beaten, and
pursued by people who wanted to harm him. He had seen miracles and conversions, but the world had not been kind to Paul.

So when he left Athens for Corinth, he arrived with a certain resignation to hold little in the way of expectations. He was weak and fearful—physically and spiritually weary. He resolved to know nothing except Christ and him crucified. This would be his spiritual food.

Paul had labored to connect with the people of Athens on their level. There he took a much more philosophical approach than he usually did in the synagogues. But the results were meager. When he came to Corinth, physically, emotionally, spiritually, and mentally beat up, he resolved to keep his approach simple. He had little reason to think Corinth would bring a response that would be any different from what he had been getting everywhere else.

Corinth was a strategic port on an isthmus that could be accessed from three directions. Port cities like this were usually commercial and cosmopolitan, populated by people from all over the world. They were also often very immoral. Corinth fit this mold, boasting a huge temple to Aphrodite, the goddess of love, complete with ten thousand temple prostitutes. So decadent was this city that the word *Corinthian* became a euphemism in those days for an immoral person, no matter where they were from. From the intellectualism of Athens, Paul moved to a city driven by materialism, immorality, and a blending of whatever religious ideas had blown into port. He braced himself.

The opposition Paul had faced up to this point was the direct result of his faithfully carrying out the mission to preach Christ. In those other cities he'd had friends with him, and their company had absorbed a lot of his discouragement. But he arrived in Corinth alone. He had seen some success in Berea, which required his companions Timothy and Silas to stay back and disciple the new believers there. This was the right thing to do. Still, it meant that Paul would have to fend for himself. When he entered Corinth he came not only looking to persuade people that Jesus was the Christ; he also came looking for work.

As a rabbi, Paul was required to know a trade. His was tent-making, so in Corinth he looked for others in his trade and found a Jewish man from Rome named Aquila and his wife, Priscilla. Aquila and Priscilla were in Corinth because Emperor Claudius was driving all the Jews out of Rome on account of a string of riots a particular group of Jews had instigated.

Paul stayed with them and worked making tents. On Sabbath days he reasoned for Christ in the synagogue. Priscilla and Aquila were among the first to believe Paul's message, which made them fast friends.

When Silas and Timothy finally rejoined Paul in Corinth from Berea, they came bearing a financial gift that the believers in Macedonia had taken up to support Paul. This money liberated him to devote himself fully to preaching about Jesus as the long-expected Messiah.

Along with the aid, Timothy and Silas also brought Paul a report of how the church was doing in Thessalonica. Though he had been able to spend only a few weeks in that city before being driven out, Paul felt a deep affection for the believers who had taken his message to heart. He worried about them learning to follow after the Lord with so little support. So as he had done for the churches in Galatia, Paul wrote the Thessalonian Christians a couple of letters, encouraging and instructing them in the faith. The first letter focused on their questions about the return of Christ and the end of the world. Paul wrote of the mystery concerning the coming of the Lord and encouraged them to live in the present, loving and serving one another with humility and diligence, clinging to the Scriptures and teachings handed down to them.

He soon had to write a second letter clarifying his first. Some had taken his words to mean that Jesus was coming back at any moment, so they had stopped working and become idle, waiting for the clouds to part and the world to end. Paul's second letter instructed them to stand firm in the faith and keep working, trusting that the Lord's timing, though unknown to them, was perfect.

In that same letter, Paul asked the Thessalonians to pray for him and his companions in Corinth. He asked them to pray that the Word of the Lord would spread and that Paul and his friends would be kept safe in the process.

This request for prayer was born not out of a hypothetical guess that his message might be unpopular. It was based on what he could plainly see. The Jews in the synagogue in Corinth reviled Paul. He had been through this many times before. Although Paul often took this sort of disdain in stride, in Corinth he protested their opposition openly, saying to the synagogue leaders, "May your blood be on your own heads. I'm going to the Gentiles from now on." Then he shook out his garments so not a speck of dust from the synagogue would go with him when he walked out.

Paul went from the public synagogue of the Jews to the private home of a man named Titius Justus, a Gentile who lived just next door to the synagogue. Many Corinthians came to believe in Jesus, including Crispus, one of the rulers of the synagogue. It seemed that Paul found greater success talking over the synagogue's back fence than in the synagogue itself. When a person wants to be heard, both his words and the context in which he delivers them have a bearing on how people listen. What Paul longed for was beginning— people were receiving Christ and him crucified. Hope was breaking into Corinth. A young church was growing, and Paul was fully devoted to shepherding it.

The ministry there was fruitful, but it was also difficult. Paul wrestled sometimes, as anyone would, with questions about how much longer he could last in his role. One night during his time in Corinth, the Lord came to him in a dream. Jesus said to Paul, "Do not be afraid. Keep speaking in my name and do not be silent. I am with you. No one will harm you or attack you. I have many people in this city." The Lord gave Paul not just inspiration but information. Paul's was not a blind faith but an informed one. God had people in Corinth. He had been at work in the city already, and now Paul was part of that plan.

Jesus' words to Paul were reminiscent of when he had told his disciples during his earthly ministry that he, the good shepherd, had "other sheep not of this fold"—Gentiles who had not yet believed but would because they already belonged to him according to his purpose. Paul would reap the harvest Jesus had spoken of back in the days before his crucifixion.

This vision and the work the Lord was doing strengthened Paul to remain in Corinth for a year and a half, serving as he was called, teaching the Corinthians the Word of God. During this time some of the Jews in Corinth tried to bring him up on charges before the Roman proconsul, Gallio, saying Paul was persuading people to worship the Lord in ways that violated God's law. Paul braced himself for how this would likely play out. He figured he would be mistreated, arrested, and jailed. Then he would be warned to stop preaching in Jesus' name and be asked to leave the city. This was the usual pattern.

But when Paul was brought to court to defend himself, the proconsul Gallio waved him off. He did not need to hear Paul's defense. Gallio found the charges against Paul trivial and undeserving of the court's time, so he threw out not just the charges but also the men who had brought them. Paul was free to go without so much as a stern word of warning.

The outcome of Paul's trial in Corinth was important. Gallio's refusal to take the charges against Paul seriously or even hear them was a huge victory for the Christians in Corinth. Gallio's ruling established a precedent for future charges brought against Christians. There, as in Philippi, a legal ruling served to offer some protection for the Christians in that town—even if it was only a little.

Paul stayed in Corinth for a long time after that, forging a deep sense of brotherhood with many in the community. Everywhere he went he developed friendships forged through trial. Every time he moved on he left most of those friends behind. This was a sad but essential part of his life as an apostle to the Gentile world.

Soon the time came for Paul to leave again—this time for Ephesus. On this occasion, however, he did not leave all of his friends behind. When he left for Ephesus, he took with him Aquila and Priscilla, his friends who had taken him on as a tentmaker when he first arrived in Corinth, broke and weary.

Paul's journey into Ephesus brought a sort of closure to his heart after having been forbidden by the Holy Spirit to enter that region a couple of years earlier. Paul had not known all those years ago why the Lord would not let him enter the Roman province of Asia. But he knew what had happened as a result. By avoiding Asia he ended up at Troas, where he crossed the Aegean Sea into Macedonia, which was the first time Christian missionaries preached Christ in Europe.

But God cared about the people of Asia too, and now Paul was free to enter. When God closes a door for a time, it does not mean that door is closed forever. So after preaching Christ and making friends in Philippi, Thessalonica, Berea, Athens, and Corinth, Paul and his companions—a group now fortified with Aquila and Priscilla—set off on a new journey for Ephesus, the main city in the Roman province of Asia.

When they arrived, Paul went into the synagogue and preached Christ to the Jews there. Many received Paul warmly and wanted him to stay. He did for a while, but eventually he longed to return to his home church in Antioch. When the time came for Paul to leave, he promised to return if God willed. But he did not leave them alone. Aquila and Priscilla stayed behind in Ephesus to assume the role Silas and Timothy had taken back in Berea—to strengthen the young church as Paul moved on.

For two years Paul, Aquila, and Priscilla had worked hard at ministry and labored together. But most roads good friends walk eventually diverge. It was God's will for Aquila and Priscilla to stay in Ephesus and for Paul to leave, so they bid each other a tearful farewell.

From Ephesus, Paul sailed to Caesarea, and from there he went up to the church in Jerusalem to reconnect with the apostles. He gave them a report of his travels and of the expansion of the church throughout the Roman Empire. It made Paul's heart glad to see some of those people who had mentored him as a new believer. Every story he told of the gospel at work was in some way the fruit of their investment in him.

After spending some time in Jerusalem, Paul went to Antioch, his home. He felt a debt of gratitude for many of the believers in Antioch similar to what he felt for the apostles in Jerusalem. Many of them had encouraged him in his early ministry.

At this point in his life, Paul had been a follower of Christ for close to twenty years. Half of that time he had spent preparing for ministry, but these most recent years had opened up the world to him. Tempered by loneliness, persecution, and pain, Paul's sense of mission and purpose to take the gospel to the Roman world only intensified. Soon, each morning when he woke up in his own bed in Antioch, he would turn his head to the west and feel that familiar longing to gather his supplies and his friends and go.

22

ARTEMIS OF THE EPHESIANS

Acts 18:23–19:41

*P*AUL ROUNDED UP HIS FRIENDS and set off again through Galatia and Phrygia, returning to cities now familiar to him because they had become filled with dear friends like Lois and Eunice, Timothy's grandmother and mother. There was a certain sweetness when Paul met up with old friends like these. His life of ministry, which early on had involved leaving new friends, now involved reunions with old ones.

When Paul came into the churches in cities like Lystra, Iconium, and Pisidian Antioch, his prayer was to build the believers up in the faith. But now they returned the favor and cared for him. It was like medicine for his soul. Following Christ meant Paul did not know where his mission would take him or what it would require of him on any given day or how it would change him. Paul had to hold everything with an open hand. His life was not his own. But through all the trials and suffering he endured, the Lord in his kindness gave Paul friends, and he loved seeing them.

In particular, he looked forward to seeing Priscilla and Aquila, who had stayed in Ephesus.

While Paul had been in Jerusalem and Antioch, a Jew named Apollos from Alexandria in Egypt came to Ephesus and began to preach Christ. Apollos was an eloquent man, trained in Greek rhetorical skills. He could take and hold an audience's attention, develop the points of his message, and do so persuasively.

He was also familiar with Scripture. He had not only studied God's Word; he understood what he studied. Sometime recently he had heard the message of Jesus from one of John the Baptist's followers, and he devoted himself to walking in the ways of the Lord. Apollos was passionate about the things of God. He taught about Jesus, though his knowledge was limited. He only knew the baptism of John—a baptism of repentance. He did not know about the Holy Spirit. But what he did know about Jesus compelled him to speak boldly and often in the synagogues.

When Aquila and Priscilla heard about him, they went to listen to him teach. He taught accurately about Jesus, but not sufficiently. So they pulled him aside and told him what they had learned from Paul and how the gospel was spreading to the Gentile world.

Apollos, with all his talents and eloquence, was humble enough to be corrected. He received Aquila and Priscilla's instruction, and as he grew in his grasp of doctrine, he also grew in his effectiveness as a preacher. He became a great asset to the church in Ephesus and stayed there for a while. But soon he wanted to go over to Corinth to help fill the gap Aquila and Priscilla had left. The church in Ephesus wrote a letter commending Apollos to the believers in Corinth, and his presence among them was a great help.

While Apollos was in Corinth, Paul took the route through Asia he had been forbidden to travel years before. The Lord had given him no such boundaries this time, so Paul went straight inland through Asia from Colossae to Laodicea to Ephesus. In Ephesus he came upon a group of about twelve new converts, but these men did not seem familiar with the Holy Spirit. They were some of Apollos's disciples. Since Apollos had not known about the Holy Spirit, neither did they. Apollos had baptized them with John's baptism of repentance, but they had not been baptized in the name of the Father, the Son, and the Holy Spirit. When Paul heard this, he baptized them all in the name of the Lord, and the Holy Spirit came upon them as he had the first Christians in Jerusalem on that Pentecost all those years ago.

Paul spent the next three months in Ephesus teaching about Christ in the synagogue. Some believed his message, but others began to resent his ministry there and tried to turn the people against him by saying evil things about Christianity. Borrowing from his experience in Corinth, Paul chose to withdraw from the synagogue, taking those who believed with him. He spent the next two years teaching daily about Christ in the lecture hall of a local philosopher named Tyrannus. Paul's message spread, and soon Jews and Gentiles from all around Asia were hearing about Christ and believing.

During this time Paul performed many miracles—healing people and casting out evil spirits. The sick and troubled flocked to Paul in much the same way people had pressed in to see Jesus in the hopes of touching the hem of his robes, or as they had done with Peter, hoping the apostle's shadow would fall on them and heal them. The Holy Spirit worked mightily through Paul so that even objects he touched brought healing. Though this was an uncommon approach for the Holy Spirit to take, it was tremendously encouraging for Paul to know the Lord was using him in such powerful ways through objects as common and profane as his sweat rags and aprons. Paul knew the power did not lie in the objects themselves but in the Spirit who accompanied them.

There was a group of seven men, professional exorcists known as the Sons of Sceva, who heard about what Paul was doing and wanted to borrow some of his fame. So when they came upon a person tormented by an evil spirit, they said, "By the name of Jesus, whom Paul proclaims, we command you to come out."

The evil spirit said, "I know Jesus, and I know Paul, but who are you?" and then proceeded to beat all seven of them until they were forced to flee, naked and wounded.

When the people heard about what happened to the Sons of Sceva, they feared the name of Jesus even more and gave Paul a new measure of respect. Many of those who made their living as charlatans pretending to be skilled in the dark arts began to confess their fraud, and some brought their sorcery books to burn in the public square. The volumes burned were together worth over fifty thousand pieces of silver. This sober response to Paul's ministry led to even more conversions.

During Paul's time in Ephesus, he got reports that the church in Corinth was struggling to live out their faith well. Corinth was a hard place to try to live as a moral person, so when he heard about their challenges, Paul decided to write them a letter addressing their struggles as well as he could from a distance. He sent Timothy and Erastus to deliver the letter, but what Timothy found was a church in upheaval, bending under the influence of those who opposed Paul. When Paul heard about this, he traveled across the Aegean Sea to pay them a visit himself.

It was a painful visit for Paul. It had cost him much personally to pour into these people's lives. After all he had done for them, their fickle hearts discouraged him. Paul spoke some hard words and called them to repent. But he did not want to push them away, so he resolved to speak his mind and then leave in order to show them mercy. Back in Ephesus, he wrote another letter calling them to repent and praying with all his heart that they would.

Paul wanted to be in many places at the same time. He saw the churches he helped plant in the way a father sees his children. He wanted to be with each of them—fully present and engaged. He wanted to parent these young believers in the faith. Even though he knew he could not do this, he felt a constant tug in his heart to leave where he was to go someplace else. It was a restlessness that would follow him for the rest of his days.

While Paul was tending to his brothers and sisters in Corinth, Christians in Ephesus became the targets of an economically motivated persecution. There was a silversmith named Demetrius in Ephesus who made his living selling idols of Artemis. The rise of a monotheistic faith was cutting into his polytheistic sales, so he gathered together the members of his guild and told them they would all lose their livelihoods if Paul was not stopped. Paul didn't just persuade people to believe in Jesus. Demetrius argued that by extension, he was persuading people not to buy the idols the silversmiths depended on for income.

"Sales aren't just drying up. Our profession is taking on a bad name. Our reputations in the community are at stake here. Even the great goddess Artemis, who is worshiped around the world, is being defiled," Demetrius said.

Panic seized the craftsmen, and they rushed into the theater in Ephesus and seized two Christian men, Gaius and Aristarchus, who were companions of Paul's, and started calling for Paul to show himself. Paul wanted to go stand with his friends. He wanted to appeal to his right to a fair trial as a Roman citizen. But when the other disciples listened to what the crowds were saying, they realized no one could agree on why they were all stirred up. One group protested about one thing, and another group about another. The only thing they could agree on—the chant that rose above the chaos for two solid hours—was "Great is Artemis of the Ephesians!" The disciples who were with Paul would not let him go in. The mob did not know what they wanted but they were hungry for justice. If Paul entered the fray he would not make it out alive.

The town clerk, an elected official responsible with keeping order, feared that his city was about to be torn apart by its own people, so he stepped forward to try to quiet the rioters. When he finally got their attention, he reasoned with them by way of a rebuke.

The clerk said, "Men of Ephesus, we all know this city is home to Artemis. And we are home to her sacred stone, which fell out of the sky. We've all seen it. No one can deny this is who we are. The world will continue to buy our statues. So be still. These men proclaiming Christ cannot take our identity away from us. They have not openly blasphemed our faith. Demetrius, you're just offended that their message is hurting your business. Fair enough. Take them to court, if you like. Bring formal charges against them, and let the proconsul do their jobs. But what we've done here today is nothing other than riot. And no one can agree on why. So please, stop this."

The crowds dispersed, and Paul found Gaius and Aristarchus unharmed. More often now, the accusations leveled against Christians failed to stand up in Roman court. The riot in Ephesus was similar to Paul's illegal arrest and beating in Philippi and his trial in Corinth, which Gallio threw out. All three situations trampled

Roman law in the name of personal satisfaction and greed. Those who respected Rome were now beginning to defend the Christians' rights to live and serve and teach openly, without being harassed. Purely emotional opposition was bad form.

The trend was encouraging, but it still highlighted the volatility of the Christians' position in the world at this point in time.

23

LOOKING EAST

Acts 20:1–21:2

P AUL WANTED TO GO TO ROME. He sensed that his opportunity
  was coming, which meant his time in Ephesus was drawing to
a close. In the past three years he had grown to love the people in
the church there. They had cared for him as much as he had cared
for them. He would miss them but he knew the time had come.

Timothy and Erastus had gone ahead of him into Macedonia, and
Paul longed to see his friends and visit the churches in Philippi and
Thessalonica again. He wondered how Lydia's and the jailer's families were doing. He could not think about his time there years
earlier without remembering the Lord's faithfulness.

Paul gathered the elders from the church in Ephesus to bid them
farewell. They had spent three difficult years together and had seen
the Lord grow the church in ways none of them could have predicted. But even more, they were friends who had surrendered their

right to their own lives for the purpose of walking in a manner worthy of the calling they had received, with all humility, gentleness, and patience. They worked to maintain a bond of peace by bearing with one another in love and in a spirit of unity and peace.

After saying goodbye, Paul headed north to Macedonia. He planned to take up a collection for the church in Jerusalem as he made his way through Macedonia and Achaia. Back when Paul had last visited the apostles in Jerusalem, they had asked him to remember the poor in their city as he traveled. The churches he would help establish would be the brothers and sisters of those struggling with poverty in Jerusalem. Paul did not forget his promise to remember the poor. Everywhere he went, he told the churches about the believers in Jerusalem and gathered whatever aid the people wanted to give to help them.

Paul had sent Titus on ahead. Titus's mission was to check on the church in Corinth and bring a report back to Paul about how they were doing. Had they received his call for them to repent and humble themselves before the Lord, or had their rejection of Paul grown worse? Whenever Paul arrived in a new city, he hoped to find Titus so that he could hear his report. Each time they arrived in a new town only to learn that Titus was not there, Paul's longing to be reunited with his brother in the faith intensified.

Paul did not find Titus in Troas or Neapolis. But one night soon after Paul and his companions arrived in Philippi, a familiar frame appeared in the doorway—Titus. Paul could see in his friend's posture that he brought good news. The church in Corinth had received Paul's call to repent with great humility and had even poured life into weary Titus, encouraging him and comforting him. They told Titus to tell Paul how much they loved him and longed to see him again.

It was as though a millstone had been lifted off Paul's shoulders. He had a deep, personal relationship with these believers in Corinth, and he had first come to them during a particularly difficult time in his ministry. He had given them his heart, and he worried that he might have lost them. But no. They looked forward to his visit, Titus told him.

Paul and his traveling companions made their way down the coast through Macedonia to the region of Achaia to the city of Corinth. The cold was coming on, so Paul and his friends settled in to winter there. During that time, Paul's thoughts often turned to Rome. Though he was still a long way from the capital city, Corinth was about as close as he ever came, so he felt it was near.

Paul knew there were already some Christians in Rome. His friends Aquila and Priscilla had recently moved back. The gospel had spread farther than Paul's reach. Wanting to care for the believers there, even if he couldn't be with them, Paul decided to write them a letter. It was the longest, most theologically thorough letter he had ever written—a manifesto about the Christian life and faith, unpacking what Christians believe, why they believe it, and how to live according to it.

He wished he could deliver his letter in person and dreamed of venturing even farther westward to Spain after spending a season in Rome. But before he could do that he needed to double back to Jerusalem to deliver the offering the churches in Galatia, Asia, Macedonia, and Achaia had collected for the poor in that city.

As the spring flowers began to color the hillsides of Corinth, Paul and his companions prepared to sail for Jerusalem. But some of the Christians in Corinth had learned that some of the Jewish leaders who opposed Paul's teaching had formed a plot to capture and kill him. So rather than sailing from the port in Corinth, Paul and his companions—Titus, Luke, Sopater from Berea, Aristarchus and Secundus from Thessalonica, Gaius of Derbe, Timothy from Galatia, and Tychicus and Trophimus of Asia—headed north, back the way they had come through Achaia and Macedonia.

When they came to Philippi, Aristarchus, Secundus, Gaius, Timothy, Tychicus, and Trophimus went on ahead across the Aegean Sea to Troas, while the rest stayed behind for a few days before joining them.

In Troas, Paul and the other believers gathered on Sunday morning to worship and pray. This was the growing custom in Christian worship—to gather on Sundays in honor of Jesus' resurrection day. Paul and his companions planned to leave for Miletus the next day, so they lingered long in fellowship with the other Christians in Troas. They shared their meals together, and Paul taught long into the night.

They had gathered in an upper room on the third floor of a house in Troas. Lamplight filled the hall against the dark outside. There was a young man named Eutychus who sat on the window ledge. He was trying hard to stay awake to listen to Paul, but he drifted to sleep in the comfort of the cool coastal breezes. He soon slumped sideways, falling out of the window three stories to the street below. The boy died on impact.

Women screamed and men gathered their robes and ran down the stairs. Paul ran over to the boy's body and lifted him into his lap and prayed. No one heard Paul's prayer above the commotion, but Paul lifted his head with a startled look and said, "There is life in him still. There is life." Eutychus jerked and opened his eyes. He looked around at the confused and teary crowd.

"Are you okay?" Paul asked.

Eutychus nodded and stood up. When everyone was satisfied that the boy was fine, they went back into the house. As they sat around the tables and talked, Paul kept an eye on Eutychus. He seemed every bit the young man he had been in those moments before he had fallen. Still, Paul watched him closely until he was satisfied too. He knew the boy had died from the fall.

Those who were gathered talked until the sun came up. When Paul stood up and began to say his goodbyes, Eutychus and his family hugged him and thanked him for his help.

<hr />

Paul sent his friends ahead of him by sea to Miletus while he stayed back in Troas for a bit. He planned to take the coastal road and make part of this return trip alone. He thought about his journey to Jerusalem and remembered that there was a moment when Jesus had set his face like a flint to that city—knowing his arrival would set in motion the events that would lead to his arrest and crucifixion. Paul believed it was an honor to suffer with Christ, and he wondered when his final journey to Jerusalem would come. Would this be that trip? He had set his face like a flint. Nothing would stop him from bringing the collection to the church there. Was this just another visit out of many more to come? Or would it be his triumphal entry?

Either way, he made haste. He moved like a man racing the clock. If he hurried he could make it to Jerusalem in time for Pentecost.

When he arrived in Miletus, Paul sent for the leaders of the church in Ephesus—his friends and colaborers in the Lord. When they arrived, Paul thanked them for their kindness and courage over the years, and he wept openly at the thought of leaving them. He loved these people and they loved him.

Paul said, "You have known me and watched my life since the first day I arrived here in Asia. You have seen my trials and my

tears. You remember how the Jewish leaders plotted against me
and how I faced so much danger while I was here. But I never held
the gospel back from you. Whatever was helpful and true, I
preached it while I was among you. Now I am going to Jerusalem,
and I don't know what will happen to me there. I just know that
the Holy Spirit has told me to go, so I'm going. The Spirit has
shown me that persecution, arrest, and affliction await me wherever
I go, so I cannot try to avoid it. Please pray that I would finish the
race with some strength left in my legs. Pray that I would not count
my life as so sacred a thing that I hold it back from God. Pray that
I would give everything I have left to proclaiming Christ and the
gospel of his grace."

The Ephesian elders surrounded him and began to pray.

Paul continued, "I don't think I will see any of you again, so I
want you to remember my words. For three years I gave you the
full counsel of God's Word. Guard your hearts and watch over the
churches you lead. You tend to a bride the Lord has purchased with
his own blood. Wolves will come in among you and try to carry off
the sheep. Watch out for them. Love your people. Never stop
telling the world about Christ and his grace. Build one another up.
Serve the weak. Empty yourselves for the sake of loving the Lord
and his bride."

Tears gathered in Paul's eyes. The Ephesian elders knelt with him
in prayer and wept together at the thought of not seeing one another again. When everyone had hugged Paul and kissed him, they
followed him to the dock and bid farewell one last time as Paul and
his companions boarded the ship headed east.

The crew untied the ropes, drew in the gangway and the loading
arms, shoved off from the dock, and steered through the harbor.
They hugged the Asian coastline for a few days, stopping in Cos and

Rhodes before landing in Patara. From there they found passage on an open-sea ship headed for Phoenicia in Syria. As the sails filled, Paul watched the land disappear behind the horizon line and turned his face to Jerusalem.

24

THE ROAD TO
JERUSALEM

Acts 21:3-17

*P*AUL AND HIS COMPANIONS sailed east passing Cyprus on their
left. Their ship was a cargo vessel headed for Tyre on the coast
of Syria before continuing on to its terminus in Ptolemais. When
the ship docked in Tyre to unload its wares and take on goods,
Paul's group sought out the local Christian community and stayed
with them for a week while they waited.

The unity these Christians found with each other, though they
were strangers, was one of the defining characteristics of their faith.
Those who shared a faith in Jesus considered one another brothers
and sisters—family. In a world filled with categories of people—
men and women, Jew and Gentile, slave and free, civilized and
barbaric, wealthy and poor—Christian people saw one another
through the lens of their shared faith based on their common need
for the mercy and grace of God.

When the Christians in Tyre heard Paul was headed to Jerusalem, they felt a check in their spirits. They warned him not to go, fearing he would only find trouble there. Paul nodded. The Holy Spirit had already made it known to him that trouble awaited him no matter where he went, and he felt the Lord was leading him to the particular trouble he would find in Jerusalem. So when the ship was ready, Paul and his company determined to continue on and went out to the docks.

The believers in Tyre followed them to the beach—men, women, and children—and knelt and prayed with the disciples in the sand. Though they only knew each other a little, the love they shared was a bond that defied time. It was a tearful parting, born out of that strange combination of affection and a sense of foreboding for what lay ahead.

From Tyre, they sailed down to Ptolemais and spent one day there before continuing on south to the port of Caesarea. This city occupied a fascinating place in the Christian story. It was home to Philip, the deacon from Jerusalem, and Cornelius, the first Gentile to believe in Jesus.

Paul's group stayed with Philip and his family for many days before heading to Jerusalem. They hoped to arrive in time for Pentecost. Philip had four unmarried daughters who all spoke the word of the Lord in powerful ways. Their family was a source of encouragement and truth for all the believers in the region.

Any time Paul stopped in Caesarea he took time to encourage the believers there. Though Paul had not personally planted any churches in Caesarea, he had played a role in establishing a Christian presence in the city. But the story of how that happened humbled him. Philip, who first brought the gospel to this town, had come as part of the dispersion of Christians from Jerusalem that took place in response to Paul's persecution. Paul's early hatred of Christianity and the stoning death of Stephen, over which he had presided, facilitated its spread. Paul was part of the reason people had to make their peace with the inherent dangers of being Christians in public. Paul had proven that this was a faith that one could be killed for.

The irony was not lost on him that he had now become one of the Christians who daily faced the possibility of death, and he was staying in the home of a man he himself had once plotted to kill.

Philip welcomed Paul and loved him. He and Paul walked the streets, rehearsing the history of this pivotal place. It was here that the Roman centurion Cornelius—the God-fearing Gentile who had a vision from the Lord to send for Peter—had come to faith. It was here that the Lord opened Peter to the idea that the gospel would spread to Gentiles without having to pass through the traditions of the Jews. It was here where Gentiles received the Holy Spirit for the first time.

Cornelius wasn't the only Gentile Christian in Caesarea anymore. Now there were many. In fact, since Peter's visit, Gentiles had been hearing the gospel and coming to faith all over the world. Most of the people in Paul's own crew were Gentile Christians.

The mission to bring the gospel to the Gentiles had its earliest roots in this city. What the Lord began there he continued through the ministry of Paul. Though Paul had become a leader in the church, his story showed that the Lord was no respecter of persons. For all of Paul's accomplishments and pedigree as a Pharisee and a scholar, there was a period in his life when he hated that which the Lord loved the most—the church, the bride of Christ. This would always be part of his story—Paul the apostle had been Saul the persecutor, and his actions all those years ago facilitated Philip's departure from Jerusalem and brought him here.

There is always mystery in the way the Lord works. No one has a simple story. Paul's friendship with Philip bore witness to that fact, and to the hope that even the most desperately lost soul can hear the call and come home.

While Paul and his company were in Caesarea, a prophet named Agabus came up from Judea to see him. Agabus was a man of good reputation who had correctly foretold the coming famine in Jerusalem several years earlier. One night at Philip's house, Agabus came over to Paul and removed Paul's belt from around his waist. In the style of the prophets of old who acted out their prophecies, Agabus wrapped the belt around his own hands and feet so that he was bound like a prisoner.

Agabus said, "This is what the Holy Spirit says, 'This is what the religious leaders of the synagogue in Jerusalem will do. They will bind the owner of this belt and hand him over to the Gentiles.'"

When the others saw this, they turned to Paul and asked him to reconsider his plans. Must he go through with the rest of this journey? Was there not another way? Why couldn't his friends take the offering to the church in his place?

But Paul had suspected this would happen before he even left Miletus. He knew this was a hazardous journey, and in every stop he made along the way people had shared his premonition. The Ephesian elders had worried about him. The Christians in Tyre had begged him not to go. And now Agabus reinforced the dread they all sensed.

Though Paul was sympathetic to their affection for him, he understood that his call was not about self-preservation. It was about pouring himself out, even if that meant unto death. So Paul raised his hand to quiet the room and said, "Listen, your weeping over me is breaking my heart. I don't want to hurt you, but what else can I do? I am not only ready to be imprisoned. I am ready to die if I must."

Before Jesus' crucifixion, Peter had made a similar statement. But back then Peter did not understand what those words meant. Paul did. They all did and they could see Paul meant what he said. When they saw that their protests put Paul in the precarious place of having to choose between pleasing God or pleasing them, they loosened their grip on him and said, "Whatever the Lord wants, may his will be done."

Those who knew the story of the events leading up to Jesus' death could not help but see the similarities with Paul's journey. He had set his face like a flint to Jerusalem and felt bound by the Holy Spirit to follow through with his plan. As Jesus had done, Paul prayed many times for the Lord to take the cup of suffering from him, but in the end he echoed Jesus, who said, "Not my will but yours be done."

Since the believers in Caesarea could not dissuade Paul from going down to Jerusalem, they opted for the next best thing—they would go with him. In the face of so many difficulties, it was this bond of unity and friendship that boosted Paul's spirit. He made the sixty-two-mile journey in the company of his friends.

When they arrived in Jerusalem, they went to the home of a believer from Cyprus named Mnason, who let them all stay with him. The Christians there happily received Paul and his companions, taking them in and telling them stories about how the Lord had been moving in their city.

Paul loved Jerusalem. Though he'd been born in Tarsus, he grew up in the Holy City. He knew this place—the way the stone streets smelled like dust and iron after a warm summer rain. He knew the way the desert winds from the east felt in the early part of the day and how the subtle scent of the sea came in on the cool western breezes of the Mediterranean in the afternoon. He knew how to pick a perfectly ripe pomegranate from a tree on Mount Zion's side, and how bread made from the grains of Bethlehem tasted in fresh olive oil from Gethsemane. He could trace in his memory the bends in the Siloam Tunnel that wound its way under the city, and the way its waist-high water from the Gihon Spring tasted when he played there as a child.

Since his time as a young rabbi studying under Gamaliel, Paul had always felt the nearness of God in this city. His life was tied to the work God was doing here, though he'd spent many years misunderstanding what the work was. Even now he knew that he saw through a glass darkly. But the Lord had taken his angry heart and filled it with love—love for the Lord and for his people.

Jesus taught that there was no greater love than to lay down your life for your friends. Paul could not help but wonder if the surge of affection he felt for his hometown was a product of the love Jesus was talking about.

PART 4

ROME AND BEYOND

AD 57–62

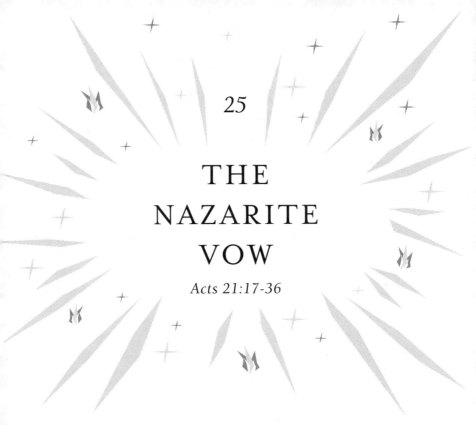

25

THE
NAZARITE
VOW

Acts 21:17-36

*T*HE NEXT MORNING, PAUL and his friends went to visit James, the brother of Jesus, who led the Jerusalem church. Many people wondered what this meeting would be like. Would it be an occasion for joy or would it be filled with tension? The reason for the question lay in the fact that, culturally, their constituencies held little regard for one another. James focused his ministry in Jerusalem primarily on Jewish people while Paul focused mostly on Gentiles.

Early on, many of the Jewish people responded strongly against the gospel, while Roman citizens tended to welcome it, so long as it didn't hurt their businesses. Paul was caught between these poles because he was both. He was a Jew and a Roman citizen—born in Tarsus but trained by Gamaliel, a prominent teacher of the law in Jerusalem. Paul was a Jewish apostle to the Gentile world.

The Jewish opposition to Christianity was evident early on in the way the religious leaders in Israel responded to Jesus himself. But it was also seen later when the religious leaders arrested Peter and John and forbade them from teaching in Christ's name. After that came Stephen's martyrdom and the subsequent persecution of all Christians in Jerusalem, which Paul himself oversaw before his own conversion. As for Paul's own experience, he had been harassed and threatened by synagogue leaders throughout Asia, Galatia, and all the other regions he visited during his travels. Paul, like Christ, had come to his own people, and his own people received him not.

With Paul not present to explain himself in Jerusalem, many of the believers there heard about his ministry and work, and they speculated about where his loyalties lay. The stories they heard depicted the Roman authorities in a rather positive light. The Gentile world seemed to welcome Paul, even calling for his help on occasion. Roman magistrates abroad honored Paul's citizenship, and even the military tribune in Jerusalem, Claudius Lysias, seemed to take a protective posture when it came to watching out for Paul and other Roman Christians.

Rome was focused on preserving the appearance of justice while the religious leaders were concerned with their own perceived theological fidelity. For Israel, this could not be guarded too closely. So even though the local believers had received Paul and his friends warmly when they first arrived in Jerusalem, Paul and company sensed an underlying tension with some of the people in the Jerusalem church. James and Paul had spent time together before during the earlier days of the church's existence, and they genuinely supported and encouraged each other in their work. But in the eyes of many, they represented two separate people groups.

As their respective movements grew, so did the questions members of their flocks raised about the other. Some in James's church wondered how far Paul had wandered from his Jewish upbringing. Had the traditions and customs of his people lost their meaning for him? Had he abandoned his Jewish roots?

To help ease this tension and establish goodwill, the first thing Paul did when he and his traveling companions met up with James was present them with the collection the churches around the Roman Empire had gathered for their brothers and sisters in Jerusalem. The financial gift was generous, but the amount was beside the point. It was a symbol of solidarity. As had been the case in the earliest days in the church when believers shared everything in common and joyfully carried each other's burdens, the church beyond the Holy City shared what they had with their brothers and sisters in need in Jerusalem.

The collection was also a symbol of indebtedness and gratitude. Jerusalem was the epicenter of the faith that had ventured out to those Roman towns. The financial gift said that though they all belonged to the same church, the Jerusalem church served as a kind of mother to the rest. Paul prayed that the church in Jerusalem would receive the gift as a genuine expression of affection. It was one thing for him to deliver it; that would be easy. It was another thing for them to receive it, which he prayed they would as a gesture of unity. To his great relief, they received the gift in a spirit of love and gratitude.

After handing over the collection of aid, Paul told James and the others what the Lord had been doing throughout Rome. He told them about persecution and the various churches that had cropped up—some of which they had been honored to plant, others of which they had only heard reports. These churches were the result of the Christian dispersion from Jerusalem after that first Pentecost following Jesus' ascension.

James and the other Jerusalem leaders praised God for what they were hearing. Joy was the only reasonable response. God was at work. The name of Christ was going out in the power of the Holy Spirit throughout the entire world, just as Jesus had said it would.

After hearing Paul's testimony, James said, "We celebrate what the Lord has done to grow his church in the Gentile world. He has also been at work here. The Jerusalem church has grown by the thousands. It is filled with people who are passionate about the law of God. Many of them have heard rumors that you teach Jews to abandon the law in order for them to live at peace with their Gentile brothers and sisters. They say you teach descendants of Abraham not to be circumcised or to circumcise their children or to walk according to our ancient customs. What shall we do about this? Surely the word is already out that you are here."

James was not concerned about what Paul taught but about how Paul was perceived. He worried that Paul's presence in Jerusalem would start trouble in the church due to his reputation as a friend of Gentiles. Not everyone approved of the decision the Jerusalem Council had made stating that Gentile Christians did not need to be circumcised. Some took this as a dismissal of the traditions the Jewish people held sacred. It was one thing not to require Jewish traditions for Gentile believers, but it was another thing altogether to tell Jewish people to abandon them. This is what many thought Paul was doing. This was a distortion of his teaching, but it wasn't hard to see how a misunderstanding like this could crop up, given the rumors people spread following the Jerusalem Council and the bias many Jewish people had against Gentiles.

For both James and Paul, it was important that the Jerusalem church receive Paul. If Jerusalem Christians could not receive him because of his association with Gentiles, they could not receive the heart of the gospel, which was all about how the grace of Christ reached beyond race or place.

Though Paul did live as a practicing Jew and knew how to fall in to Jewish company and customs, it was also true that he spoke up whenever he heard about Gentiles being pressured to take on Jewish customs in order to express their Christianity. Nothing should be added to the finished work of Christ for salvation, he said. Nothing. Freedom in Christ meant relying on his grace alone for salvation— not on religious traditions or rituals.

For Paul, this freedom cut two ways. It didn't just mean Gentiles were excused from observing Jewish traditions. It also meant Jewish Christians were free to continue practicing them if they wanted.

But the rumor in Jerusalem among many believers there was that Paul taught against this—that he wanted Christians to abandon all Jewish traditions and customs. James recognized this as a problem and so did Paul. If this was the prevailing view, people would not only refuse to listen to Paul, they would dismiss what he was doing and as a result miss a key part of their own faith—that the gospel was meant to go out to the farthest reaches of the world, drawing believers from every tribe, tongue, and nation.

James proposed a solution. There were four men in the Jerusalem church who had just taken on the Nazarite cleansing ritual. This ritual involved a season of fasting and prayer, during which the celebrants refrained from cutting their hair. Since Paul had been away from Jerusalem for so long and had no doubt made himself ceremonially unclean according to the Levitical code, James suggested that he possibly join these four men and go through the ceremonial cleansing with them—and maybe pay the way for all five of them with his own resources. If he did this, people would see that he had not distanced himself from his Jewish upbringing. It would be a sign to all that Paul still respected the Jewish way of life.

Paul conceded to James's request and went to the temple the next day to give official notice that he was going through the ceremonial purification and would return in a week to complete the ritual. There were no theological grounds for Paul's participation in this ceremony except that of caring for the consciences of his brothers and sisters. The Nazarite vow was familiar to Paul. He had actually gone through it five years earlier in Corinth. Here in Jerusalem it was an act of humility—an outward sign of gratitude to God and respect for his people. And it was a gesture of cultural sensitivity he and James hoped would open people up to what he had to say about Christ and his gospel.

But his act of deference caught the attention of many Jewish unbelievers in the city who opposed not just association with Gentiles but Christians as well. With Pentecost drawing near, Jerusalem was beginning to fill with pilgrims. Some Jews from Ephesus came to worship at the temple—men who had heard about Paul's ministry in their city. These men were committed to punishing Paul, given the chance, for his willingness to associate with Gentiles. Earlier that day, they spotted Paul with an Ephesian man they also recognized—a Gentile convert named Trophimus. When they saw Paul again in the temple area later that day, they assumed Trophimus was with him. Incensed that Paul would bring a Gentile into the temple, the men from Ephesus started to cry out to the other people in the temple, pointing at Paul and accusing him of defiling their holy place. "This man teaches people to reject the law of God, and today he has brought a Greek into our sacred space!"

These two accusations—that Paul would defy the law of God and defile the temple—brought pious retribution. The religious worshipers surrounded Paul, seized him, and dragged him out of the temple, locking the door behind him. Outside the temple doors, the people began to beat Paul with the intent to kill him. News of the upheaval made its way to the military tribune whose job was to maintain peace in the temple, especially during the holy feasts.

Fearing the angry mob would become a riot, the captain of the guard took a cohort of soldiers and centurions and ran into the crowd and stopped the beating. They bound Paul in chains and led him out of the courtyard, saving his life. The tribune asked the crowd what Paul had done to deserve this harsh treatment, but some shouted one answer and others another.

The crowd did not calm down. They demanded Paul's blood. This was another instance of Roman justice protecting Paul from bloodthirsty religious fervor. To save Paul, the tribune knew he needed to arrest him. It would not be safe for the apostle to walk free at this point. So the tribune had his men carry Paul up the steps to the barracks and keep him out of reach of the mob.

When the crowd saw him being carried away, they cried out, "Away with him!"

Paul saw the barracks entrance and he wondered: once that door closed behind him would he ever walk the streets of Jerusalem again as a free man?

26

THE PLOT TO KILL PAUL

Acts 21:37–23:35

AS *PAUL WAS ABOUT TO BE TAKEN* into the barracks he asked the tribune, Claudius Lysias, for permission to address him. The captain was surprised to hear him ask this in Greek. He said, "You speak Greek? I thought you were the Egyptian revolutionary who has had this town upset. You're not him?"

Paul said, "You mistake me for someone else. I am not him. I am a Jew from Tarsus—a city you know. I'm begging you, please let me speak to the people."

Lysias looked at him for a moment and, with a wave of his hand, granted Paul's request. Paul stood on the steps in front of the barracks and motioned with his hand for the people to quiet down to listen to him. They did.

In Hebrew, Paul said, "Brothers and fathers of Jerusalem, please allow me to make my defense."

His use of Hebrew quieted the crowd even more.

"I am a Jew. I was born in Tarsus in Cilicia, but I was raised here in this city. I studied the law of our fathers under Gamaliel. I was as zealous for the law of God as you are right now. I considered myself a protector of the faith. When followers of Jesus of Nazareth made themselves known, I persecuted them. I was committed to finding and destroying every last one of them—men and women alike. Ask the high priest and his entire council if you want. They will tell you this is true. They wrote letters sanctioning my work as a destroyer of the Way.

"Then one day, as I was on my way to Damascus to arrest Christians there, at around noon, when the sun was at its brightest, a great light appeared and shone down on me, blinding me. I fell to the ground and heard a voice from the sky saying, 'Saul, Saul, why are you persecuting me?'

"I was helpless, so I called out in my blinded state, 'Who are you, Lord?' The voice said, 'I am Jesus of Nazareth, whom you are persecuting.'

"The people who were with me saw the same light, but they did not hear what I heard. They just saw me in the dust, asking, 'What do you want me to do, Lord?'

"I heard Jesus say, 'Get up and go into Damascus. I will tell you what to do then.' So my friends led me into the city, and soon a Christian man named Ananias came and found me, at the Lord's prompting. He stood in front of me and said, 'Brother Saul, open your eyes and see.' As sure as I can see you now, my sight returned then.

"Then Ananias said, 'The Lord has called you to himself. He has appointed you to know him and be his witness in the world. Stand up and be baptized. Call on his name.' So I went back into Jerusalem, and as I was praying in the temple, I fell into a trancelike state and saw Jesus of Nazareth saying to me, 'Get up and leave this place. People here will not accept your testimony about me.'

"I said, 'Lord, why would they not listen to me? Shouldn't I, of all people, have a voice among the Jews? After all, they know I was the one who persecuted Christians. They know I beat people who believed in you. They know I approved of Stephen's death. Won't my testimony be persuasive on account of that?'

"But the Lord told me again that I would not have a voice in that place. He told me I was to take the message of Christ away from here and out into the Gentile world, which I have done."

Up until this point, the crowd had been listening carefully, wondering where Paul would take his story. Would he try to explain that he was a friend of Jewish people everywhere? Would he claim there had been some misunderstanding?

But when Paul said the Lord had called him to leave a deaf Jerusalem for a hearing Gentile world, they became enraged. When they heard this they began to call out for him to be taken away. They said, "This man deserves to die!" and started throwing their garments and dust and stones at him. Lysias knew they only had seconds before this became a full-scale riot, so he took Paul inside the barracks and ordered that he be examined by flogging—a torture method trusted to quickly compel a prisoner to tell the truth.

As they began to stretch Paul out with ropes tied to each hand, he said to the centurion binding his wrist, "Has it suddenly become legal for you to flog an uncondemned Roman citizen?"

The centurion stopped what he was doing and saw that Paul was serious. The centurion went and told Lysias what Paul had said. The tribune came to Paul and asked, "Are you a citizen of Rome?"

"I am," Paul said.

Lysias said, "So am I. It cost me a fortune, but I bought my citizenship. And you?"

Paul said, "I am a citizen by birth."

When he said this, the entire guard stopped what they were doing. One soldier stepped forward and unbound Paul. They placed him in a cell overnight in order to keep him safe but also to figure out what to do with him. They still did not understand why the people were so upset. They figured the best way to find this out would be to bring Paul before the Sanhedrin so the tribune could hear straight from the source. The next morning, Lysias called the Sanhedrin to assemble for him, and he brought Paul to stand before them.

The council could not disguise their hatred for Paul, but Paul stared them down for a moment before saying, "Brothers, some of you know me. Up to this day I have lived my life in good conscience before God."

The high priest commanded one of the guards near Paul to strike him on the mouth. A rush of anger surged through Paul. He said, "God will strike you down, you whitewashed wall! You pretend to judge me according to your law and then violate it by ordering this soldier to strike me?"

The council members were taken aback by Paul's audacity. They said, "Do you dare rebuke the high priest?"

Leveraging the irony of the moment, Paul said, "Was it really the high priest who ordered the guard to strike me? It never occurred to me that a man of such prestige would issue such an order. Well, since I am commanded to never speak ill of one of my rulers, I do apologize."

Though he could not make out who everyone was in the room, he sensed some were Pharisees, who believed in a bodily resurrection, and others were Sadducees, who did not. He said, "Brothers, listen. I am a Pharisee. I am the son of a Pharisee and was raised by Pharisees. I am on trial because of my belief in the resurrection from the dead."

This caused the Pharisees and Sadducees in the room to begin to argue with each other. Paul did not start the debate. It had been going on for years. But when he threw a little fuel on that fire, the argument grew sharp and tempers ran hot. Before long the Pharisees in the room were calling for his release, on the principle alone that he sided with them. The debate became violent, and Lysias feared the council would tear Paul in two. So he commanded his soldiers to get him out of there and take him back to the barracks.

Paul was relieved that he made it out of the Sanhedrin alive, but as he sat in his cell that night, anxiety whispered dark words into his heart. He knew his situation was serious and that he could not deflect the Sanhedrin's anger for long. Then a familiar presence came into his cell—one he had known before. The Lord Jesus stood with him.

Jesus said, "Take heart, my servant Paul. I told you that you would testify about me before kings, and so you shall. As you have testified about me here in Jerusalem, so shall you bear witness to me in Rome."

Paul longed to bring the gospel to Rome, but it was beginning to dawn on him that he would likely do so as a prisoner.

The next day, a group of more than forty Jewish leaders gathered to discuss how to deal with Paul. His presence in Jerusalem threatened to divide the people during Pentecost. They determined that he needed to be put to death, one way or another, and bound themselves by oath to neither eat nor drink until Paul was dead. Then they went to the chief priests and elders and told them about their vow. They said, "Here's what we want you to do. Tell the tribune that you want him to bring Paul back to us. Tell him you want to convene a proper trial. Then when Paul comes in, we will kill him."

Paul's sister's son overheard the plot and ran to tell Paul about it. Paul summoned one of the centurions and asked him to take the boy to Claudius Lysias. "He has something important to say."

When Lysias learned that the boy had news, he took him aside, and the boy told him how the council was going to ask for another trial with Paul, and how there were more than forty men lying in wait with the intent to kill this Roman citizen under Lysias's charge.

Lysias told the boy not to tell anyone that they had talked and sent him on his way. Then he called for two of his most trusted centurions and said, "Go assemble two hundred soldiers, seventy horsemen, and another two hundred spearmen. Prepare them to travel to Caesarea this night. Also, prepare horses for Paul and his companions. Take him safely to Governor Felix."

Then Lysias sat down to pen a letter to the governor. He wrote:

From Claudius Lysias, to his excellency, the governor Felix. Greetings. This man I'm sending was apprehended by the Jews in Jerusalem, and they were about to kill him before I arrived, rescued him, and took him into my custody. He is a Roman citizen. When I inquired about the charges the Jews had against him, I learned they were religious matters that do not warrant death or imprisonment. When I learned today that the Jews had made a plot to kill him, I sent him to you at once. I have ordered his accusers to come to you to make their case further.

Lysias's soldiers marched under cover of darkness with Paul and the letter to Antipatris thirty-five miles outside of Jerusalem. The next morning the foot soldiers returned to Jerusalem while the horsemen took Paul the rest of the way to Caesarea, where they delivered Lysias's letter to Felix and then handed over Paul.

Felix read the letter and looked up at Paul. "What province are you from?" he asked.

Paul said, "Cilicia."

Felix nodded and said, "I will give you a hearing when your accusers arrive." Then the governor told his guards to put Paul in Herod's praetorium to await his trial.

27

BEFORE FELIX
AND FESTUS

Acts 24:1–25:12

*F*IVE DAYS AFTER *PAUL WAS SENT* to Herod's praetorium in Caesarea, Ananias, the high priest in Jerusalem, arrived, along with several other members of the Sanhedrin and their legal counsel, Tertullus. Tertullus formally submitted their case against Paul to Governor Felix, who agreed to give them a hearing.

When the court convened, Tertullus stepped forward to make the Sanhedrin's argument. He opened with customary remarks of flattery. Tertullus told the governor how grateful they all were for Felix's leadership and how his reforms were splendid and helpful to all.

The truth was that relations between the Jews and the Romans were growing increasingly strained the longer Rome occupied the Promised Land. Though Felix knew their praise was empty, their deference carried some value. His ability to maintain peace during troubled times was a sign of strength in the eyes of those who had the power to promote him. So even if the Sanhedrin did not genuinely appreciate Felix and his leadership as much as they professed in this moment, Felix received their willingness to say things that misrepresented reality as a sign of the respect he required.

This was all Tertullus wanted anyway. He hoped to gain some of the governor's favor through flattery before trying to gain his confidence concerning the merits of their case, which he knew were weak.

Tertullus said, "We wish to detain you no longer, so please allow me just a brief moment to explain our case."

Felix nodded and Tertullus pointed at Paul and said, "This man is a plague. He is a public nuisance. He infects people's minds. He stirs up riots among the Jewish people. I know you read Claudius Lysias's letter, your excellency. This man caused the riot Lysias had to shut down. He is guilty of sedition. Not only that, he is also the ringleader of a sect devoted to Jesus the Nazarene, and he is known for causing disturbances among the Jewish people all over the Roman Empire."

Felix considered these two charges in light of his legacy. Would it be wise to release a man who stirred up trouble? Certainly Paul's message had aroused the anger of Jewish leaders around the empire, but this was not his objective. It was an outcome of his ministry, never a motive.

Tertullus then brought a more specific charge. "We apprehended this man while he was in the process of trying to defile the temple by bringing a known Gentile into the court reserved only for Jews. We frustrated his attempt, but he would have done it. Most excellent Governor Felix, we are confident that when you examine him, you will see for yourself that our charges are both true and significant concerning the peace of Jerusalem."

At this, the members of the Sanhedrin affirmed everything Tertullus had said.

Three charges stood against Paul. He was a threat to Roman
peace. He was a Christian. And he had deliberately attempted to
defile the temple. The governor nodded to Paul, inviting him to
speak in his own defense.

Paul rose and addressed the governor.

"Knowing that you have judged this nation with wisdom and
prudence for several years now, I happily make my defense to you,
your excellency. Ask around in this very city of Caesarea and you
will find witnesses who will verify I was here less than two weeks
ago. I have not been in Jerusalem for any length of time. And if
you ask around in Jerusalem you will find witnesses who will
testify that I never went into the temple to argue with anyone. I
did not stir up any crowds—not in the temple, not in the synagogues, not in the city itself. No one can offer you a shred of proof
that I profaned the temple."

The absence of proof offered little comfort to Felix. The truth
was that Paul was causing a disturbance with the high priest of Jerusalem, and the proof of that was right in front of his eyes.

Paul continued, "As for their second charge, I am a Christian. My
accusers call it a sect, but I worship the God of our fathers, and I
believe everything that is written in the Law and the Prophets. I
share with many of my accusers a hope in the resurrection of the
dead, and with all of them that there will be a reckoning for both
the just and the unjust. I have taken pains in my life to live in such
a way that I have a clear conscience before God and man. I was
away from Jerusalem for several years. Knowing the struggles they
faced with the famine, I collected aid for my brothers and sisters in
the Holy City in every town I visited.

"The reason I was in Jerusalem this past week was to deliver that offering and to present myself for purification in the temple. This is what I was doing when some men from Asia caused the uproar that has me before you today. Where are those men who brought this third charge of trying to defile the temple anyway? Shouldn't they be here if it is on account of their indictments that I am on trial?

"My accusers here have not witnessed any of the chargeable offenses they bring against me. Ask them, your excellency, what they have seen me do. Ask them what laws they saw me break when they had me arrested in Jerusalem. The only thing I did to cause a stir was make it known I was on trial because I believed in the resurrection. But I didn't start that debate. The council chose to divide itself over that topic, not over me."

Governor Felix was more familiar with Christianity than he let on. There were believers in Caesarea. He knew them by reputation. It was evident to the governor that none of the charges against Paul could be substantiated. He wanted to release Paul and be rid of the whole thing, but he also wanted to preserve the respect of the Jews who had the power to promote dissatisfaction with his governing style. He decided to put the whole thing off by saying he would make his decision after conferring with Lysias.

Disappointed, the Sanhedrin members went back to Jerusalem. Felix told his guards to hold Paul in custody but to do it in the way they would hold any uncondemned Roman citizen awaiting trial. Paul was treated well and given a measure of freedom. His friends were permitted to visit him, bring him food, pray with him, and take care of any needs that might arise.

Not too many days later, Paul was surprised to learn that Felix and his wife, Drusilla, had come to visit with him. They wanted to talk about Christianity. Paul spoke to these two with the same conviction he used everywhere else. They talked about justice and self-control—both relevant matters for the governor. Then Paul brought up the Lord's coming judgment. Both Drusilla and Felix felt the weight of Paul's words, to the point that Felix abruptly ended the conversation, saying he would come back to talk more at a later time.

Drusilla was interested in Christianity. As much as Felix might have shared her curiosity, his mind would drift back from time to time to the offering Paul mentioned gathering for the believers in Jerusalem. Was there more somewhere, he wondered? Over the course of the next two years, Felix left Paul in prison and came to visit him many times. They talked about Paul's faith, but Felix hoped their conversation would one day turn to the topic of a bribe. Repenting and following Christ was too expensive of a venture for Felix, but Paul's freedom was something he was certain the apostle could afford. He hinted at this often. Paul could buy his freedom if he wanted.

Paul never took the bait. Instead, the two men got to know one another over those two years. Felix gave Paul vague assurances that his case was still in process, but when the time came for Felix to yield his post to the incoming governor, Festus, Felix's desire to remain on good terms with the Jews prevailed, so he left Paul in prison for Festus to deal with.

The Jews in Jerusalem knew they were getting nowhere with Felix, so they had stopped trying. But once Festus assumed power, they came to him and asked him to hear their case against Paul anew. They wanted him to execute justice.

Three days after Festus took power, he went up to Jerusalem. The chief priests laid out their case against Paul and asked Festus to summon the apostle to Jerusalem for trial there. They did not actually want a trial. They still planned to ambush him along the way and kill him before he ever arrived.

Festus told them he would be returning to Caesarea soon. They could come with him and try Paul's case there. If they had a case, Festus promised to act on it.

The following week Festus returned to Caesarea and Paul's accusers went with him. On the morning after they arrived, Festus took his seat in the tribunal and ordered his centurions to bring Paul before him. When Paul came into the room, he saw his accusers—some familiar faces who had been there two years earlier, and some new faces of young Pharisees learning how to argue a case in a Roman-occupied Israel. They immediately began to restate the charges they had brought against Paul previously, and they introduced a couple of new vague and baseless offenses as well.

Paul offered the same defense he had given before, appealing to Festus, saying, "I have not committed any offense—not against the law of the Jews, not against the temple, and certainly not against Caesar."

As it had been with Felix, Porcius Festus was more concerned with being on the right side of things with the Sanhedrin than he was with Paul, so he said, "If the charges are as baseless as you say, would you like me to take you to Jerusalem to try your case there?"

A flicker of confusion came across Paul's face as he took in what Festus had just proposed. Festus wanted to kick him down to a lower court. His confusion quickly gave way to indignation. Paul said, "If you are asking what I want, let me tell you. I am standing before Caesar's tribunal now. This is where I ought to be tried. I have done no wrong against the Sanhedrin. You know this is the case. Felix knew this too. If I have done anything that warrants death in the eyes of Caesar, I will not try to escape that fate. But if there is no basis for the Sanhedrin's charges against me, no one has the legal authority to hand me over to them. I am a Roman citizen. I appeal to Caesar."

Festus smirked a little at the providence that had just fallen into his lap. He would not have to hand Paul over to the Jews, and neither would he have to deal with him in his own court. Festus conferred with his tribunal and said to Paul, and everyone else there, "To Caesar you have appealed; to Caesar you shall go."

28

BEFORE HEROD AGRIPPA II

Acts 25:13–26:32

N*OT LONG AFTER HEROD AGRIPPA I* died after beheading James and imprisoning Peter, his young son Herod Agrippa II assumed a small portion of his kingdom. Agrippa II was the great-grandson of Herod the Great, who had tried to find and kill the infant Jesus. Agrippa II was only seventeen when his father died, so he was considered too young to take over as king. But since he was the king's son, he was given a small territory in the northern part of the kingdom to rule.

Herod Agrippa II came from a long line of kings, and with that heritage came deep roots in paranoia and self-preservation. So when Festus became the new governor, Agrippa decided to travel to Caesarea to welcome his new colleague to his post and make an impression that would inspire Festus to honor him.

Agrippa and his half-sister Bernice arrived in Caesarea a short time after Paul appealed to Caesar. Festus told Agrippa about this strange prisoner Felix had left him. He said, "I was in Jerusalem not too long ago, and the high priest and members of the Sanhedrin laid out their case against him. They strongly urged me to condemn him to death. I told them it was not customary to condemn a man before he had a chance to defend himself in front of his accusers. I brought them back here with me and the following day took my seat on the tribunal and ordered his hearing.

"But when Paul's accusers stood up to explain why he deserved to die, they didn't make any sense. I thought they would have some sinister case against the man, but all I really heard from them was jealously and petty rage. Their anger at him was connected to this Nazarene man named Jesus. I believe Pontius Pilate introduced this Jesus to your father. Neither Pilate nor your father thought he did anything deserving death, but the Jewish leaders demanded it, so Pilate crucified him. My prisoner claims that Jesus rose from the grave and is the Lord of a new sect."

Herod Agrippa II nodded. He was familiar with this Jesus, and he was also intrigued by the complexity of Festus's predicament.

Festus continued, "Honestly, I am at a loss for how to proceed. On hearing the case, I didn't think Paul deserved to be condemned. But his accusers persisted, and I didn't want to upset them by a perceived lack of due process. So I asked the prisoner if he wanted to go to Jerusalem to face his accusers there in a trial over which I would preside. Do you know what he did? He appealed to Caesar. He said the Jewish court was a lesser court and asked for a trial before the emperor of Rome instead. I have him in a cell in the praetorium right now. My men are making preparations for his journey to Rome as we speak."

Agrippa was fascinated by this story. It did not follow the predictable path of a man trying to obtain his freedom.

Agrippa said, "I would like to see this man. Would you permit me to hear from him myself?"

Festus said, "Yes. Tomorrow if you like."

The next day, Agrippa and Bernice came to the tribunal in all their royal splendor and entered the court with the other dignitaries and prominent men of the city. Once they had all taken their seats, Festus brought Paul into the hall.

Festus said, "King Agrippa, and all who have honored this hall today, this is the man the Jews in Jerusalem and here in Caesarea keep petitioning me to condemn. I have not found that he has done anything deserving of death, but he has appealed to Caesar. I have decided to go ahead and send him, but I am struggling to figure out how to explain my reason for doing so. I have invited you here to listen to the case, examine the man, and help me decide what to write to the emperor concerning why this man now stands before him. It is, you would agree, unreasonable to send a prisoner to stand before the emperor without clearly naming the charges against him."

The court was amused by Governor Festus's predicament. Festus was caught in a political quandary of his own making. Not wanting to upset the Jewish religious leadership, he was reluctant to release Paul. But that local political decision now required that he prepare a defense for the ruler of the entire empire. Political quandaries like this were inevitable for anyone governing in Rome. But for middle managers like Festus, they often found themselves stuck between the people they governed and the rulers they reported to. Mishandling a case like Paul's could ruin Festus's career and legacy.

Agrippa nodded at Paul and said, "You may speak."

Paul stepped forward, raised his hand, and said, "I consider myself fortunate to stand before you today, King Agrippa. I know you are familiar with Jewish custom and law, so please, allow me to make my defense against these charges the Jews in Jerusalem have brought against me.

"I grew up in Jerusalem, in and around the temple. The fact that I am a part of Israel and that I grew up in Jerusalem is known to every one of my accusers. If they had the integrity to testify, they would tell you that I lived the strictest life of observance to the law possible. I was a Pharisee. And I now stand trial because of my hope in the promise God made to our forefathers—that God would raise the dead and keep us with his everlasting love. Since the days of Abraham this has been our people's hope, and yet for this hope I now stand accused.

"Not too long ago, O King, I was convinced that I should oppose any who claimed the name of Jesus the Nazarene. And I did. I persecuted Christians in Jerusalem. I arrested some, and I voted for the stoning of others. The court that accuses me now sanctioned my persecution then.

"I was an effective persecutor, even beyond the city of Jerusalem. But one day, as I was going to Damascus to arrest Christians there and bring them back to Jerusalem for trial, with papers in hand from the chief priests endorsing my work, I saw a light come down from heaven, brighter than the sun. It blinded me. I fell to the ground and heard a voice call out to me in Hebrew, saying, 'Saul, Saul, why are you persecuting me?'"

Paul was practiced at telling this story. He told it with all the drama it deserved, but he also measured his words so that it would not sound so fantastic that his hearers would think him insane and stop listening. Paul told Agrippa about his encounter with Jesus and how he heard the Lord call him to proclaim the resurrection of the dead through faith in Jesus to the Gentile world. The Lord had called him to open the eyes of the spiritually blind so they might turn from darkness and live in the light of forgiveness.

Paul then said, "O King Agrippa, I did not disobey the voice. How could I? I went first into Damascus and told the believers there what had happened to me, and then I went to Jerusalem and did the same. Soon I was traveling all over the regions of Galatia, Asia, Macedonia, and Achaia, calling people to repent of their sins and turn to God through faith in Jesus. This is why the Jewish leaders in the temple seized me and tried to kill me two years ago."

As a king with Jewish roots, Agrippa understood some of the complexity of what Paul was saying. The prisoner claimed to honor the same Scriptures the Jewish rulers said he opposed. He claimed Jesus was the fulfillment of God's covenant promises, which the chief priests saw as heresy. Agrippa found Paul's resolve and courage fascinating.

Sensing he had the king's full attention, Paul said, "Through all of this I have known the peace and presence of God. I stand today before kings and common people with nothing new to say but rather something ancient. I proclaim what Moses himself said would come to pass: that the Messiah must suffer and die, and by being the first of his kind to rise from the dead, would proclaim light both to our people, the Jews, and to the nations."

Festus felt his face flush with embarrassment. These were not the words of a sane man. He stood up and said, "Paul, you are out of your mind. You are clearly an educated man, but your great learning is driving you insane."

Paul said, "I am not out of my mind, most excellent Festus. What I'm saying is both true and reasonable to someone who knows

Jewish law. His honor, King Agrippa, is familiar with the teachings of which I speak—the customs of Israel. That is why I am speaking so freely to him. I trust that he has followed my logic. I have hidden nothing in my meaning."

Paul turned to Herod Agrippa II and said, "You believe the prophets, don't you? I know you do."

Paul's direct manner caught the room off guard. Common people did not address the king with such impertinence, much less a prisoner bound in his court.

Not wanting to let Paul control the conversation, Agrippa said, "What are you trying to do here, Paul? Persuade me to become a Christian too? Now? Do you think you've won me over here in this short time?"

Paul said, "Whether it happens now or years from now, my prayer is that you and everyone in my hearing would become what I am, minus these chains."

Paul raised his wrists and rattled the shackles that bound him. He meant what he was saying. Everyone could see that. Paul sincerely hoped that everyone in that court—whether then or in the near future—would hear Christ's call to repent. This was the heart of the case against him—he wanted people to put their faith in Christ, not in ritual or custom. He was not trying to take over the temple. He was not trying to lead an insurgence. He was not trying to defy Caesar. He was trying to call people to repent of their sins. As offensive as this might have been to a person's ego, it was not a crime.

King Agrippa, Governor Festus, and the other dignitaries gathered left the court and went into Festus's chambers. Agrippa said to Festus, "This man has done nothing deserving imprisonment or death."

Festus nodded. He knew.

Agrippa said, "It's a shame, really. We could set him free right now had he not appealed to Caesar."

Acquitting a Roman citizen who had been granted a hearing before the emperor was considered an offense against king and country—a circumvention of justice. For Agrippa, Paul's appeal to Caesar was a technicality that kept the apostle bound. But for Paul, it was turning out to be a shrewd strategy that brought him one step closer to Rome.

29

SHIPWRECK

Acts 27:1–28:10

O NCE FESTUS MADE PREPARATIONS to send Paul to Rome, he placed the apostle and some other prisoners in the care of a centurion named Julius, who would escort them to the reigning Caesar in Rome, Nero. Julius put his charges on a ship from Adramyttium, which was scheduled to skirt the coastline of Asia, stopping in Sidon and then in Myra in Lycia. Luke and Aristarchus were permitted to travel with Paul, along with a few other companions.

In Myra, Julius secured passage on a ship carrying grain bound for Italy. He and his prisoners sailed slowly along the Asian coast. The weather was rough and the seas choppy, making the journey slow and precarious. When they drew near to Cnidus, the southern winds pushed against them as they slowly fought their way south to Crete. They sailed under the leeward shelter of Crete's southeastern coast and made it as far as Fair Havens on the southern side of the island before they had to stop.

The journey so far had taken longer than they planned, and they were getting into the dangerous winter season. When the sailors wanted to press on for Italy, Paul said to the ship's captain, "Sir, if we press on, I fear we will suffer for it. Cargo will be lost. Men will die. We're past the sailing season."

But Julius deferred to the captain and the owner of the ship—both of whom wanted to press on at least to Phoenix on the southwestern tip of Crete. Fair Havens was not a suitable place to harbor for the winter. If they could make it down the coast just another forty miles west they would have safe harbor in Phoenix where they could reassess.

While they were weighing this decision, the north winds died down and a gentle south wind came along, opening what appeared to be a window of time for safe passage down to Phoenix. The crew, soldiers, prisoners, and Julius the centurion readied the ship, raised their anchors, and set off. But before they could reach Phoenix, a great northeaster swept down the mountains of Crete, pushing the ship away from the island. Caught in the tempest, the sailors had no choice but to yield to the wind and let it carry them out to sea. They hoped to catch a bit of refuge in the shelter of the nearby island of Cauda.

Cauda provided just enough relief for the crew and the prisoners to raise, drain, and secure on board the small boat used to transport people from ship to shore and to connect some undergirding cables used to support the main vessel's hull.

The seafaring men knew they were at the mercy of the winds and prepared themselves for open sea. The Sands of Syrtis, which lay to the south of Crete and just north of the Libyan coast, were never far from the sailors' minds. Dreaded by all who sailed the Mediterranean Sea, this shoal was a boneyard of ships that ran aground. Though they knew Syrtis lay well to their south, they also knew those sands only made their presence known by grabbing the hull of a ship, stranding it in the hidden shallows until the wind and waves pushed it deeper into the reef. When this happened, few passing vessels would risk a rescue attempt for fear of meeting the same fate.

The sailors dropped their drag anchor to slow their speed and tried to keep the ship as steady as possible. When the wind persisted and battered the ship throughout the night and on into the following day, they began to jettison cargo to lighten the vessel. The next day, they threw the beam that held the mainsail and its tackle overboard as well, hoping to make themselves a smaller target for the winds. They got rid of anything the storm could grip hold of— anything they could afford to lose and a few things they could not.

The storm persisted for the next eleven days. The sea was violent and the sky was overcast both day and night. The crew lost their bearings, unable to navigate by sun or stars. A feeling of gloom spread throughout the boat. Many of the men began to count themselves lost. Hope of rescue seemed a cruel gamble.

Every night Paul prayed for the Lord to calm the sea. And night after night the storm raged on. Then one night while he was praying in the surging, makeshift barracks below deck, an angel of the Lord appeared to Paul and said, "Do not be afraid, Paul. No one with you will die because God has appointed for you to stand before Nero."

Paul gathered the men on the ship and said, "You remember that I predicted this storm would fall upon us. The same God who gave me the premonition about the storm sent one of his angels to assure me that we will all survive this journey. The angel told me we would run aground but will not die. So take heart. I will stand before Caesar. My life will be preserved, and since you are with me, so will yours. I am confident of this."

On the fourteenth day of the storm, after many days lost in the Adriatic Sea, the sailors heard the telltale sound of breakers in the water and knew they were close to land. At midnight, they took a sounding and measured twenty fathoms. Then, after some time had passed, they took another sounding and measured fifteen fathoms. They let down the anchors to slow the ship and prayed for daylight so they could see what lay before them. The sailors confirmed to each other that this might be their only opportunity for rescue. But they did not have enough boats to ferry everyone on board to land. There were over two hundred people on the ship. The sailors began to lower the ship's boat, claiming they just wanted to use its anchors to add to the drag, but Paul knew they were planning to abandon the ship.

Paul went to Julius and said, "If these sailors leave in that boat, we will never see them again. If they leave, you and your men will die."

Julius ordered his men to cut the rope that tethered the boat to the ship. The sailors watched in horror as the small boat drifted away, and Julius gave them a look that said, "Now what?"

The sailors had been found out and they knew it. They could make no protest, so they returned to their work on the only ship they had left.

Before dawn, the weather began to die down and a hint of morale began to return to the men on the ship. The crew wanted to lighten the vessel even more. They decided they would scrub their mission altogether and dump their grain. But the men had not eaten a proper meal in days, so Paul urged everyone to eat their fill first.

He said, "You need your strength. Not one of you is going to die."

Then he took bread, blessed it in the presence of the entire ship, broke it, and ate it in the manner of Christ's last supper. His prayer and encouragement lifted the passengers' spirits, and soon everyone began to eat their fill—Christians, Jews, Greeks, and Romans alike. Conversation and laughter soon filled the air. As men began to entertain the possibility of hope, dawn broke over the horizon. The ship's crew gave orders to throw the remaining wheat overboard into the sea.

As they heaved the sacks into the water, they saw land in the distance—a bay with a beach. They did not recognize the island but were grateful for it nonetheless. They decided to aim for the beach, sail as far as they could go until their battered ship ran aground, and swim the rest of the way. They cut away their anchors, loosened the ropes that locked the rudders together, hoisted the foresail, and made for shore.

While they were still some distance away, they struck a sandy reef and lodged there. The bow was stuck. They could not move forward and they could not go back. The surf beat against the sides and the ship's stern began to come apart. They needed to abandon ship, and they needed to do so quickly. The soldiers discussed what they should do with the prisoners. If any escaped under their watch, the soldiers might be put to death themselves. One suggested they kill the prisoners to prevent any from escaping. But Julius objected. He needed to keep Paul alive. He needed to take Paul to Rome. This soldier was committed to his mission, and if he was being completely honest, he also felt a sense of indebtedness to Paul. If Paul's words were true, Julius was alive because of this prisoner. Killing the man who saved him would be bad form.

Julius ordered those who could swim to jump into the water and make their way to shore. For those who couldn't he told them to grab hold of wreckage from the ship floating in the water and use whatever they could find to make for land. No one would die that day. Not if Julius could help it. Still, he was amazed to discover that once everyone had abandoned the ship and crawled up on the beach, not a single person was unaccounted for. Not one.

Soon people from the island came to assist the castaways. They told the shipwrecked men they had landed on Malta. They took them in and made a fire for them because the night was cold and they were wet.

As Paul went to put a bundle of sticks he had gathered on the fire, a viper emerged from the pile and latched onto his hand. The islanders saw the viper and knew Paul would be dead within minutes. Knowing he was a prisoner, they assumed he must have been a murderer to deserve such a fate. But Paul shook the snake off into the fire and kept about his work.

The Maltese people watched him, wondering when he would swell up and fall down. But Paul remained unfazed by the serpent's bite. Seeing this, the islanders began to believe he was a god. No one survived a bite from that particular snake. When they asked Paul what sort of a man he was, he smiled and told them he was not a god. He was a man who had an appointment with Caesar.

The chief of the island, a man named Publius, received the shipwrecked men and showed them gracious hospitality. Paul learned that Publius's father was sick with a fever and dysentery. The apostle asked if he could visit the man and pray for him. Publius agreed and brought Paul to where his father lay dying. Paul put his hands on the old man and prayed, and Publius's father was instantly healed. The chief thanked Paul through his tears. When others heard what had happened, those with diseases came to Paul and each one was cured.

The island people cared for the men from the ship and tended to their needs while they wintered together for the next three months, until the seas were once again safe.

30

ROME AT LAST

Acts 28:11-31

*A*FTER THREE MONTHS, near the beginning of March, the seas
became safe once again for travel. Julius took his prisoners to
the port of Malta on the other side of the island. There they found
a grain ship from Alexandria that had made it safely to Malta and
chosen to winter there. The prow of the ship was adorned with the
gods of the constellation Gemini—Castor and Pollux, the twin sons
of Zeus and Leda, protectors of the seafaring and gods of navigation.

The ship sailed north to the major shipping port city of Syracuse
on the eastern shores of Sicily. They docked there for three days
before sailing on to the city of Rhegium on the southernmost tip of
Italy's boot. The ship did not plan to stay in Rhegium long, and
when a southern wind came along the following day, they quickly
made their preparations and sailed up the western coast of Italy to
the city of Puteoli, a major port in the Mediterranean wheat trade.

Puteoli, like any port city, was made up of people from all over
the world. It was home to every race and creed. When Paul and his
friends stepped off the ship with their faithful centurion guard,
word quickly spread to the Christians in the region that the apostle
Paul was in their town. A small group representing the believers in
Puteoli came to Paul and invited him and his traveling companions
to stay with them. Julius agreed to this, and Paul, Luke, Aristarchus,
and Julius spent the following week with their Christian hosts. As
word of their arrival spread, believers from as far as the Forum of
Appius and the Five Taverns came down to meet them. These villages were on the road to Rome, and these Christians wanted to
accompany the apostle on the final leg of his journey.

Though many of them had never met Paul, they all felt a debt of
gratitude to the man. Many of them had heard the gospel of Jesus
Christ from people who had heard it from Paul. The phenomenon
of the gospel was that in such a divided world it made strangers
into brothers and sisters, people bound to each other in this life
and the next.

Their company was tremendously encouraging to Paul. He had
hoped and prayed that his labor was not in vain, and though he
never believed it was, seeing all these brothers and sisters in Christ
coming to be with him connected how his life and ministry had
made its way to them. This sense of connection helped put what
awaited Paul in Rome in its proper place. Even if he died, his life of
ministry would live on and continue to spread. He had friends in
the capital city of the greatest empire in the world. He would not
be alone.

After the week in Puteoli, Paul and his companions were taken
to Rome. Believers from the area joined him as he traveled. When
the Eternal City first came into view, Paul stopped to take it in. Here

lay the ends of the earth. What came into Rome went out into the world. He felt like a cross between a native son and a smuggler. He had known himself to be a Roman citizen his whole life. This was a point of personal pride and a robe of protection. But now, concealed in his mind and heart was a doctrine that would change the world, and no one could strip it from him.

Rome, with all her ambition, with all her assassinated rulers who lay dead under the dripping daggers of their closest friends, with all her aspirations toward peace undone by her commitment to war, was an empire in desperate need of mercy and grace. She needed to die and rise again. She needed Christ and him crucified. This was what Rome needed more than anything else. Though the ruling class didn't realize it, this was why Paul was so determined to come to her—even if it meant he would arrive in chains. Even if it meant he would never leave.

When they entered the city, Julius processed his prisoner. Since the centurion had never known Paul to be a threat or an escape risk, he arranged for Paul to live on his own, under the supervision of a soldier. When Julius's work was done, he came to tell Paul goodbye. The centurion had spent close to half a year escorting this man through land, sea, storm, and shipwreck to face trial for crimes some believed made him deserving of death and others believed were no crime at all. Julius was not Paul's judge, but he could not dismiss the fact that were it not for his prisoner's faith, he would be lying somewhere on the bottom of the Adriatic. Paul said a prayer for his guard's safe passage home and bid Julius an affectionate farewell.

After three days, Paul sent out a request asking the leaders of the synagogue in Rome to come to where he was under house arrest. It was his custom to reach out to the Jewish leaders in every new town he visited. Rome was no exception, though his situation was exceptional. These leaders, perhaps even more than the Roman authorities, had the influence to see Paul released. If they heard from him and found no reason for him to be in chains, their opinion would certainly carry weight with the Romans, who had little interest in settling religious disputes.

When a sizable group had gathered at the apostle's house, Paul said, "My brothers, I come to Rome as a prisoner from Jerusalem. The leaders of the synagogue there wish for Rome to execute me. But I have done nothing deserving death. I have done nothing against our people or against the customs of our fathers. I promise this is true. But I was nonetheless arrested in Jerusalem and handed over to the Romans. When Governor Felix, Governor Porcius Festus, and even Herod Agrippa II examined me, they found no basis for the charges against me and wanted to set me free. They could neither substantiate nor make sense of the charges the leaders in Jerusalem brought. But because the Jewish leaders in Jerusalem persisted and plotted to kill me, I had to make my appeal to Caesar to avoid their trap.

"Know this: I have not come here to bring charges of my own against Israel. I have no accusation to make against my own people. If you will indulge me, I would like to explain myself to you. I was sent to Rome because of my belief that the great hope of Israel, the Messiah, has come. It is because of my loyalty to Israel's hope, not my betrayal of it, that I am in these chains."

The synagogue leaders listened to Paul, weighing his words. One of them said, "We know nothing about your situation. We have heard of you, but we have received no letter from Judea discussing your case. We have not even come across anyone speaking evil against you in this matter."

Paul knew this would likely be the reality. The leaders in Jerusalem knew their case would only weaken the farther it traveled from Judea. Since their case against Paul lacked credible witnesses and coherent charges, no one was surprised that the Jerusalem leaders didn't try to prosecute Paul any further after he was taken away.

The synagogue leader continued, "We would like to hear from you, however. We are very interested in what you have to say, because even though we are unfamiliar with your case, we know Jews throughout Rome who speak against the sect to which you belong, which has a church here in Rome. Let us gather our leadership and return at a later date so you can explain what this is all about."

The Jewish leaders and Paul set a time for when they would come back with the rest of their colleagues to hear him explain what he believed. When that day came, a large number of local synagogue leaders came to Paul's house. That morning and on into the night Paul proclaimed the gospel. He did not use this opportunity to address the merits of his legal case. Instead, he wanted to persuade them to believe in Christ. If they did that, he won everything that mattered to him anyway.

Paul based his teaching on the books of Moses and the prophets of old, showing how their messages pointed to the person and work of Christ. Paul opened the Scriptures and taught the synagogue leaders about Jesus from their own texts. The Word of God was, by necessity, the word of his appointed Messiah. If Jesus was indeed that Christ, then his ministry was not a distortion of the Jewish faith but its fulfillment. The Christ had ushered in a new age, and the kingdom of God had become known by her king's mercy.

Some of the Jews who heard Paul believed his teaching. But as it happened whenever Paul expounded the Scriptures to religious leaders, many rejected his message as well. Those who were persuaded by Paul got into an argument with those who were not. In an effort to regain the room, Paul raised his hand to speak. The debate died down and Paul stood up.

He said, "The Holy Spirit was right when he spoke to your fathers through the prophet Isaiah. He said, 'Tell the people they hear, but they never understand. They see but never perceive because they have let their hearts grow hard to the truth. They shut their ears and close their eyes. But if they would open them, I would let them see. If they would listen, I would cause their hearts to understand who I am to them and who they are to me. I would turn and heal them.'"

The synagogue leaders knew Paul was pronouncing judgment over them. His words warned that if they continued to refuse to be open to the Word and work of God, there would come a point when they would forfeit the ability to receive anything from the Lord.

Paul said, "Let it be known, sirs, that the gospel I proclaim about the Messiah our fathers longed to see is a message of salvation that goes out to the Gentiles too. And they will listen. They will see and hear."

This never failed to be a jarring statement. That God was interested in Gentiles at all was an untenable thought for many traditional Jews. But for others, they could not dismiss the notion out of hand because the God they knew was a merciful, searching God. He had been merciful to them. Why would he not also be merciful to others?

Still, the mention of Gentiles being included in God's covenant never failed to stir debate and divide a room—and this moment was no different. Soon Paul's guests were debating the place Gentiles could hold in the plans of God.

The argument between those who believed Paul and those who did not took over the meeting, but as the day grew late, the debate grew halfhearted. Soon the crowd began to thin as people went back to their homes.

After that meeting, some of the synagogue leaders came back to hear more from Paul. Others simply dismissed him. But in those early months, no one pressed hard for the prisoner's death. Paul spent the next two years living as a prisoner under house arrest in Rome. He paid his own way through tentmaking and through the generosity and kindness of other Christians. He was under the constant watch of a soldier; sometimes he was chained to his guard, other times not. But Paul continued his work as an evangelist for the Christian faith. Though he could not travel, many people heard about him and came to his house to listen to him teach with their hearts, ears, and eyes open. He welcomed all who came to him and continued preaching Christ and him crucified.

Paul also used this time to write. He wrote several letters to churches throughout the Roman Empire—some of which are preserved today in the canon of the New Testament. Others have been lost to time.

There were days when Paul's spirits were high and others when he felt the constraint of his imprisonment as a deep sorrow in his soul. But in a letter to his young son in the faith, Timothy, who was becoming a revered pastor in his own right, Paul wrote, "Remember Jesus Christ, Timothy. Remember him risen from the dead, the son of David. Remember him as I proclaimed him to you in the gospel for which I am now suffering, bound in chains as a criminal. Timothy, remember. The Word of God is not bound. I endure everything for the sake of those who would believe, that they would find salvation in Christ Jesus and join him in his eternal glory. Trust these words:

> If we have died with him, we shall live with him also;
> And if we endure this life, we shall reign with him in glory;
> If we deny him, he will deny us,
> But if we are faithless, he remains faithful because he cannot
>   deny himself."

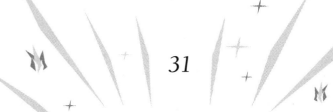

31

ON EARTH AS IT IS IN HEAVEN

Philippians 1:18-30

MUCH OF WHAT ULTIMATELY HAPPENED to the central figures of the early church is unknown or unclear. Scripture and early church historians help piece together the puzzle.

James the Just, the brother of Jesus, led the church in Jerusalem for many years. Though he did not accept Jesus as the Messiah prior to the resurrection, James and Jesus' other brothers all came to believe after Christ was raised and gave their lives to building the church. Though his brothers went out as missionaries, James felt called by God to serve the church in Jerusalem. The Epistle that bears his name is thought to be one of the earliest letters to circulate, meaning it would have stood alone for a period of time as many people's only written explanation of the Christian life.

James died as a martyr. One early church historian described his death like this: "The Scribes and Pharisees placed James upon the pinnacle of the temple and threw down the just man, and they began to stone him, for he was not killed by the fall. And one of them, who was a fuller, took the club with which he beat out clothes and struck the just man on the head."

Barnabas continued on as a missionary for the gospel of Jesus Christ, taking his cousin John Mark with him on a second mission to Cyprus. Six years after Barnabas and Paul parted ways over John Mark's decision to leave their first missionary journey, Paul mentioned Barnabas as his still-active colaborer for Christ. Though they were not together in body, they remained together in mission. Early church historians hold that Barnabas was martyred and that John Mark witnessed his cousin's death and buried him privately.

John Mark resurfaced in Scripture ten years after leaving Paul. Interestingly, it was Paul himself who mentioned him in his letter to the Colossian church, asking them to welcome John Mark when he came, not as Paul's assistant but as one of his fellow laborers. During Paul's imprisonment in Rome he asked Timothy to bring John Mark when he came because he was useful to him. Peter also benefited from John Mark's service and counted him as a son. Mark went on to write the gospel that bears his name, and the early church historian Eusebius said Mark became an evangelist in Egypt, founding a church in Alexandria over which he became the bishop.

Titus, known for his diligence and dependability, also continued working as a missionary. Paul charged him to strengthen the churches through doctrinally sound teaching and good works, and he told Titus to appoint elders in every city he visited. Later, Titus took the gospel to Dalmatia (present-day Croatia), where he lived out the remainder of his days.

Timothy, Paul's dear son in the faith, led the church in Ephesus and also traveled to tend to Paul during his Roman imprisonment. Paul

commended Timothy often as an example of Christlike character—
humble, gentle, and teachable. Early records suggest that Timothy
became the first bishop of Ephesus, and his remains were later
interred in the Church of the Apostles in Istanbul.

Luke stayed with Paul during his imprisonment in Caesarea
and Rome, not only to care for the apostle but also to gather
stories and doctrine for the books he was writing—the Gospel
bearing his name and the Acts of the Apostles. As a writer, Luke
showed remarkable command of the Greek language. He also
cared deeply about historical accuracy. Along with being a writer,
some traditions hold that he was a painter. Some believe Luke was
martyred, while others say he died from old age at eighty-four
while living in Greece.

Onesimus and Philemon reconciled. Scholars believe the fact
that Paul's letter to Philemon was preserved and distributed among
the churches indicates that Philemon did receive Onesimus back as
a brother, freed him, and then sent him back to minister alongside
Paul, as Paul had requested. Some historians believe Onesimus
himself went on to become the bishop of Ephesus fifty years after
his conversion, taking over for Timothy.

After John and Peter were arrested in the temple in Jerusalem
for preaching Christ, they both continued to lead as pillars in the
Jerusalem church until the Lord led them on to works in other
places. John served the church in Ephesus for a season before
being exiled to Patmos by the Roman Emperor Domitian, who
reigned from AD 81–96. In Patmos, John had the vision he wrote
about in Revelation. After Domitian's death, it seems John returned to Ephesus. He wrote the Gospel bearing his name, three
epistles, and the book of Revelation as an old man, all during the
last quarter of the first century. John was the only one of the

original twelve disciples to die of natural causes. Judas took his own life, and the other ten were martyred.

Peter was crucified by Nero in Rome around AD 64. He asked to be crucified upside down because he did not count himself worthy to die in the same manner as his Lord. When Peter left the Jerusalem church in the faithful hands of James, he went out as a missionary in much the same way Paul had. Around the time Nero came to power in the early AD 60s, Peter arrived in Rome. There he preached about Christ and helped Mark write his Gospel. He also wrote two epistles bearing his own name during that time. Rome's great fire of AD 64 happened not long after Peter's arrival. Rumors spread that Nero had started the fire so that he could rebuild the city for his own glory. Needing a scapegoat, Nero pinned the blame on Christians and began to persecute them mercilessly. Many Christ-followers were rounded up, crucified, and set on fire to light up the city streets. Peter died during this persecution.

As for Paul, it seems his case was heard and he was acquitted, which he equated with being rescued from the lion's mouth—likely a reference to Nero. Historians do not agree on exactly what happened next, but many concur that Paul continued to minister in Christ's name and was arrested again not long after his release. His second imprisonment seemed to intensify as the months passed. One friend, a Christian from Ephesus named Onesiphorus, came to Paul's aid. He did not conceal the fact that he was looking for Paul, and when he found him he took care of him. Onesiphorus's courage to seek out the imprisoned apostle was a balm to Paul's heart. The political climate in Rome, especially after Nero took power, did not favor Christians.

Soon, however, Paul was martyred by Nero—same as Peter.

For all of this, history sees through a glass darkly. The details may be hard to pin down, but the net effect is that every key player in the early church suffered, and most of them died for their faith.

Though much of what happened to the apostles after Peter and Paul's imprisonment in Rome is unclear, here is what we do know. The resurrection of Jesus Christ opened a door between the fallen, groaning world into which he was born and the renewal of all things. That door was a stone rolled back by the very finger of God from the mouth of a grave outside of Jerusalem.

The risen Jesus not only gave his people new life, he gave them each other. He put them together into a community of faith where they would live, move, and have their being under the mercy of their gracious king who would call them his beloved bride—the one for whom he would return. He sent his Holy Spirit to live inside their hearts to cultivate in them a boldness, humility, and unity that would make them more into a single thing than a collection of individuals. Together they would be the church—the radiant, beloved bride of Christ.

After the resurrection, Jesus' disciples lived the remainder of their days laying down their lives for the sake of making known his gospel. But what came from them, through the power of the Holy Spirit, was a movement that spread like a fire around the world and continues even now. As it is with any global movement of transformation, the changes began not with politics, land, or armies, but with individual people embracing a particular faith held together by some basic tenets that make up orthodox Christianity.

What are those foundational beliefs?

People are saved by grace through faith in the Son of God. This was a central theme not only in Paul's preaching but in the entire body of Scripture. The law of God proved that humanity could not keep it. Historically, God calls to himself stiff-necked people, and

Christ died for the ungodly. The message of the cross of Christ is that God gives faith to the faithless, grace to the transgressor, and life to the spiritually dead, all by grace through faith in the Son of God.

The Holy Spirit, who attends to God's people in these latter days, lives in those who follow Jesus. The presence of the Holy Spirit bears witness to the lordship of Christ. Jesus promised that the Spirit would come after him and that the presence of God would transfer from a temple built by human hands to human hearts created by God himself. The Holy Spirit illuminates the truths of God in the hearts of his people—revealing things into which angels long to look. The Holy Spirit is the guarantee, the "down payment," of the Christian's eternal adoption into God's household and the redemption of our bodies. The indwelling Holy Spirit joins God's people together as a single body and destroys the dividing walls that separate people from each other.

Those who place their faith in Christ are made new. They are transformed into new creations, made one by the finished work of Christ. Believers in Jesus are baptized in his name into a local fellowship with other believers. Together they walk in this new life, living out their days in the community of faith until Christ returns. All human divisions that separate us from each other are erased in Christ. There is no more Jew and Gentile, slave and free, male and female. All who believe are one in Christ. Believers in Christ are those who once walked in darkness but have since been brought into the light of God's truth.

There is great mystery in every facet of this story. Whenever humanity tries to understand the things of God, we cannot help but anthropomorphize the unsearchable. We have no option but to try to understand the transcendent ways of our eternal God through earthbound images, concepts, and words.

But even though God is mysterious, he has chosen to be knowable. He has given us his Word, told largely as a story, with poetry and teaching woven throughout. He has worked in time and space through politics and kingdoms, but also through an unassuming virgin and lowly fishermen, to make himself known and accomplish his will. He has parted seas and raised the dead. He has comforted the afflicted and afflicted the comfortable. He has commissioned his people to proclaim his grace and has gathered them to himself when they have died for it. He has called and preserved a people for himself, from every tribe, tongue, and nation, and they are scattered across the globe, down through time even now. They are an imperfect people, full of ambition, fear, and poor judgment. They do not point to the goodness they obtain in Christ nearly as often as to their need for the forgiveness and redemption he gives.

But they remain. She remains—the bride of Christ.

After all that has happened—from the fall of man to the covenant of grace God cut with Abraham in which he promised to never forsake his people, from the Babylonian and Assyrian exiles to coming home to a Roman-occupied state, from the birth of Christ to his death and resurrection, from his ascension to the spread of his gospel throughout Jerusalem, Judea, Samaria, and the ends of the earth—the enduring mystery of faith remains. What is that mystery?

Christ has died. Christ has risen. Christ will come again.

We live between two advents.

ACKNOWLEDGMENTS

*T*O THE FOLLOWING I owe a debt of gratitude:

Lisa. Thank you for walking through this life with me. Though it is short, you make it rich. I love you.

Jane, Kate, Margaret, and Chris. You guys are the best. I am a better man for knowing each of you. Thanks for cheering me on. I love you.

Rick and Susan Ramsey. Ryan and Nancy Ramsey. Nathan and AJ Durham. This book has its roots in where and how I was raised. I am glad I grew up around you.

Andrew Peterson, A. S. Peterson, and Justin Taylor. Thank you for supporting my writing over the years. This book would not exist without your help. I am deeply grateful.

Amanda Bible Williams, Raechel Myers, and the entire team at She Reads Truth / He Reads Truth. Thank you so much for giving me a place to work with the words and truths of Scripture every day.

Bethany Jenkins. Your continual encouragement and support has been a great gift. I appreciate it. Thank you.

Andrew Osenga. I cherish our friendship. Thank you for reminding me that making art is supposed to be fun.

Leif Enger. I am still looking for glimmering things. I'm happy to report they are everywhere. Thanks for supporting my writing. I draw so much inspiration from yours.

Scott Sauls and the entire team at Christ Presbyterian Church. Thank you for recognizing my call to pastor and for giving me such an amazing church to call home.

Al Hsu, my editor. Lori Neff, Alisse Wissman, Krista Clayton, and the rest of the team at InterVarsity Press. Kristi Reimer, my copyeditor. I heard someone say recently that getting a book published is nothing short of a miracle. Thanks to each of you for the roles you play. It has been an honor working with you.

Andrew Wolgemuth. Thanks for being my agent and for curating so much of my creative work. Let's keep doing this. It's fun.

NOTES

18   *Perhaps the synagogue ruler*: Luke 8:40-56.

18   *Lazarus, whom Jesus had also raised*: John 11:1-44.

18   *Former lepers*: Luke 17:11-19.

18   *newly sighted blind people*: Matthew 21:14.

18   *once-paralyzed beggars*: Matthew 15:30.

18   *God had made them to need*: Genesis 2:18.

18   *These were people who had come*: 2 Corinthians 12:19.

19   *Judas Iscariot, who had betrayed*: Matthew 27:1-10; Acts 1:15-20.

19   *Scripture told them*: Psalm 69:25; 109:8.

3 PENTECOST

21   *Since Israel's early days*: Leviticus 23:17.

21   *Pentecost also commemorated*: Exodus 19-24.

22   *That had not been the case*: Genesis 11:1-9.

23   *They would perform signs*: Joel 2:28-32.

23   *Then Peter told the crowd*: Isaiah 53:11.

23   *David had written*: Psalm 16:10.

23   *The Messiah would be seated*: Psalm 16:8-11; 110:1.

25   *They lived believing*: Luke 12:15.

25   *They embraced the idea*: Matthew 20:28.

4 FLEE TO GOD

30   *They had not understood*: John 1:36.

30   *As for Peter*: Matthew 26:75.

30   *Some of you acted*: Luke 23:34.

31   *God himself would put*: Isaiah 53:5-6.

31   *That city would protect*: Joshua 20.

31   *Their sins would be forgiven*: Acts 3:19.

31   *Pray for Christ to return*: Acts 3:21-26.

5 PRAYER FOR BOLDNESS

33   *In the morning the Sanhedrin*: Matthew 26:1-6, 57-68; 27:1-2.

34   *When they deliver you*: Matthew 10:19-20.

36   *Why do the nations plot*: Psalm 2.

6 ANANIAS AND SAPPHIRA

40   *May I be in them*: John 17:20-23.

40   *Since the days of the first sons*: Genesis 4:1-16.

41   *Barnabas reasoned that if God*: Romans 8:32.

42   *See how these Christian people*: Attributed to North African theologian Tertullian of Carthage (AD 155–240), *Apologeticum* 39, 7.

44   *People were free to give*: 2 Corinthians 9:7.

7 GAMALIEL'S WAGER

47   *To whom shall we go*: John 6:68.

8 STEPHEN AND SAUL

54   *God's design for the sons of Abraham*: Genesis 17.

56   *Lord, receive my spirit*: Luke 23:46.

56   *He was a Pharisee among Pharisees*: Philippians 3:4-5.

57   *Father, forgive them*: Luke 23:34.

9 PHILIP

59   *be his witnesses in Jerusalem, Judea, Samaria*: Acts 1:8.

60   *For faith to be saving*: Ephesians 2:8.

61   *Nevertheless Philip rose*: Psalm 84:10.

61   *Like a sheep he was led*: Acts 8:32-33; Isaiah 53:7-8.

62   *Philip and the eunuch*: Matthew 28:19.

63   *he was legally forbidden*: Deuteronomy 23:1.

63   *Your seed shall inherit*: Isaiah 54:3.

63   *Let not the foreigner*: Isaiah 56:3-4.

10 DAMASCUS ROAD

68   *Then the light flashed again*: Acts 26:13.

70   *There on the Damascus road*: Galatians 1:15-21.

72   *The apostles received Saul*: Galatians 1:18.

72   *Peter told Saul*: John 6:1-14; Matthew 14:22-36.

73   *This time he returned*: Galatians 1:22.

11 WHAT GOD HAS MADE CLEAN

74   *Before Joshua's conquest*: Exodus 25:8; Exodus 36–39.

74   *after Israel took Canaan*: 1 Kings 6.

75   *worship in spirit and in truth*: John 4:23-24.

75   *It had been a destination*: Psalm 122:1-2.

76   *They watched in total astonishment*: Mark 5:35-43.

77   *God worked wonders*: 2 Corinthians 12:12.

77   *It was Jesus himself*: Mark 3:13-19.

78   *The Lord God has heard*: Matthew 25:34-40.

13 BARNABAS AND PAUL IN ANTIOCH

89   *there were many localized famines*: Josephus notes this in *Antiquities*, 20.2.5; cf. 20.5.2 and 3.15.3.

91   *Lord, do you want us to call down fire*: Luke 9:51-56.

91   *On another occasion he and John*: Matthew 20:20-21.

92   *Jesus gave these brothers a nickname*: Mark 3:17.

14 PRECIOUS IN THE SIGHT OF THE LORD

93   *He was a walking contradiction*: John 21:15-17.

94   *What is that to you?*: John 21:18-22.

94   *Reports of this conversation spread*: John 21:20-23.

94   *Jesus had already told*: Mark 10:38-39.

94   *their deaths were already known*: Psalm 116:15.

94 *Jesus alone had the words*: John 6:68.

95 *A story later circulated*: Eusebius, *Church History* 2.9.

97 *It is a fearful thing to fall*: Hebrews 10:31.

98 *His robes were woven with silver*: From Josephus's description in *Antiquities* 19.8.2.

99 *His attendants ran to his side*: From Josephus's description.

15 A Diverse and Sending Church

105 *A subtle shift occurred*: Acts 13:46, 50; 15:2, 22.

105 *This would become their pattern*: Romans 1:16-17.

107 *John Mark's decision bothered Paul*: Acts 15:38.

107 *He outlined how Old Covenant*: Acts 13:16-25.

107 *Jews in Jerusalem had not recognized*: Acts 13:26-31.

107 *Christ was the fulfillment of specific prophecies*: Acts 13:32-37.

108 *Paul concluded his message*: Acts 13:38-39.

108 *not to dismiss the gospel message*: Acts 13:40-43.

109 *They did not see that the law*: Romans 2:27.

16 There and Back Again

114 *As he rode by*: Matthew 21:6-11.

114 *But only a few days later*: Matthew 27:15-23.

115 *They talked about the coming trials*: Acts 14:22.

115 *They nurtured these congregations*: Acts 14:23.

17 The Jerusalem Council

119 *Paul and Barnabas both jumped*: Ephesians 2:8-9.

120 *From his perspective*: Acts 10.

121 *all the Gentiles who are called*: Amos 9:12.

122 *Paul promised to remember*: Galatians 2:10.

123 *You are a Jew*: Galatians 2:11-14.

123   *There was no Jew or Greek*: Colossians 3:11.

123   *To show favoritism to the Jews*: 1 Timothy 5:21.

124   *We know a person is not justified*: Galatians 2:15-20.

18 COME OVER AND HELP US

125   *Paul wrote a letter*: Paul's Epistle to the Galatians.

127   *How could Barnabas*: Colossians 4:10.

127   *Son of Encouragement*: Acts 4:36.

127   *Barnabas set sail for his hometown*: 1 Corinthians 9:6.

127   *John Mark continued to proclaim*: Colossians 4:10; 2 Timothy 4:11.

129   *So even though Paul*: This sentence is adapted from a statement about Paul by John Newton, *The Thought of the Evangelical Leaders*, Notes of the Discussions of the Eclectic Society, London, during the years 1798–1814, ed. John H. Pratt (1856; repr., Banner of Truth Trust, 1978), 151.

129   *He made up his mind*: Romans 14:13.

129   *Ever since he had put his faith*: Luke 1:1-4.

129   *And he was equally interested*: Acts 1:1-5.

130   *Conversion never comes just through hearing*: 1 Thessalonians 1:6.

130   *Her house became the center*: Acts 16:14.

19 THE PHILIPPIAN PRECEDENT

132   *a demon-possessed man who followed Jesus around*: Mark 1:24.

20 CONCERNING THE UNKNOWN GOD

138   *Paul's preaching was blessed*: 1 Thessalonians 1:5.

138   *Some received it eagerly*: 1 Thessalonians 2:13.

138   *Believers there tried to model*: 1 Thessalonians 1:6-7.

138   *The Thessalonian church contributed*: 1 Thessalonians 1:8.

140   *Paul considered himself a citizen*: Colossians 1:21-23.

140   *He wasn't shocked to see*: Acts 17:16.

142   *The question that had always troubled*: Romans 1:18-23.

143   *God is not far from any*: Acts 17:28-31.

21 THE ROADS GOOD FRIENDS WALK

146   *He resolved to know nothing except*: 1 Corinthians 2:2-3.

147   *Aquila and Priscilla were in Corinth*: F. F. Bruce, *Paul: Apostle of the Heart Set Free* (Grand Rapids: Eerdmans, 1977), 381.

147   *When Silas and Timothy*: 2 Corinthians 11:8-9.

147   *The first letter focused*: 1 Thessalonians.

148   *He soon had to write*: 2 Thessalonians.

148   *He asked them to pray*: 2 Thessalonians 3:1-2.

149   *Jesus' words to Paul*: John 10:16.

150   *Paul's journey into Ephesus*: Acts 16:6.

22 ARTEMIS OF THE EPHESIANS

155   *The sick and troubled flocked*: Luke 8:43-48.

155   *hoping the apostle's shadow*: Acts 5:15.

156   *Paul decided to write them*: 1 Corinthians.

156   *He sent Timothy and Erastus*: 1 Corinthians 16:10-11.

156   *a church in upheaval*: 2 Corinthians 2:1; 7:8-13.

157   *But he did not want to push*: 2 Corinthians 1:23-24.

157   *Back in Ephesus, he wrote*: This letter is lost to time, but it is referred to in 2 Corinthians 2:3-4.

23 LOOKING EAST

161   *They worked to maintain a bond*: Ephesians 4:1-3.

161   *Back when Paul had last visited*: Galatians 2:10.

161   *Each time they arrived*: 2 Corinthians 2:12-13.

161   *They told Titus to tell Paul*: 2 Corinthians 7:5-6.

162   *It was the longest, most theologically thorough*: Paul wrote his Epistle to the Romans during this winter in Corinth.

162   *But before he could do that*: Romans 15:23-25.

163   *Lamplight filled the hall*: Acts 20:8.

164   *He thought about his journey to Jerusalem*: Luke 13:31-35; Isaiah 50:7; Luke 9:51.

164   *Paul believed it was an honor*: Philippians 3:8.

164   *If he hurried he could make it*: Acts 20:16.

165   *I don't think I will see*: Acts 20:18-35.

24 THE ROAD TO JERUSALEM

167   *In a world filled with categories*: Romans 12:2.

168   *The Holy Spirit had already*: Acts 20:23.

168   *Any time Paul stopped in Caesarea*: Acts 18:22.

169   *Though Paul had become a leader*: Acts 10:34.

170   *Agabus was a man of good reputation*: Acts 11:28.

170   *In the style of the prophets of old*: Isaiah 8:1-4; Jeremiah 13:1-11.

171   *Listen, your weeping over me*: Acts 21:13.

171   *Before Jesus' crucifixion, Peter*: Luke 22:33.

171   *Whatever the Lord wants*: Acts 21:14.

171   *Not my will but yours*: Luke 22:42.

172   *He could trace in his memory*: The Siloam Tunnel, known today as Hezekiah's Tunnel, is not only a water source for Jerusalem, drawing from the Gihon Spring, it is also a popular place for children to explore, and has been for centuries.

172   *Even now he knew*: 1 Corinthians 13:12.

172   *Jesus taught that there was no greater*: John 15:13.

25 THE NAZARITE VOW

175   *Early on, many of the Jewish people*: Acts 19:23-27.

176   *But it was also seen later*: Acts 4:1–5:42.

176   *Stephen's martyrdom*: Acts 7:54-60.

176   *Paul himself oversaw*: Acts 8:1-9:23.

176   *Paul, like Christ, had come*: John 1:11.

176   *The Gentile world seemed to welcome*: Acts 16:6-10.

176   *Roman magistrates abroad*: Acts 16:25-40; 18:12-17.

176   *even the military tribune*: Acts 21:31-36; 22:22-29.

177   *As had been the case in the earliest*: Acts 2:42-47.

177   *Paul prayed that the church in Jerusalem*: Romans 15:31.

177   *These churches were the result*: Acts 23:1-13.

178   *The name of Christ was going out*: Acts 1:8.

178   *We celebrate what the Lord has done*: Acts 21:20-22.

179   *Though Paul did live as a practicing*: Galatians 4:10-11.

179   *If this was the prevailing view*: Philippians 2:9-11.

179   *Nazarite cleansing ritual*: Numbers 6:1-21.

180   *He had actually gone through it*: Acts 18:18.

180   *This man teaches people to reject*: Acts 21:28.

181   *The tribune asked the crowd*: Acts 21:31-33.

181   *Away with him*: Acts 21:35-36.

26 THE PLOT TO KILL PAUL

186   *Take heart, my servant Paul*: Acts 9:15.

27 BEFORE FELIX AND FESTUS

191   *reckoning for both the just*: Daniel 12:2.

192   *He wanted to release Paul*: See the story of Pilate and Jesus in Luke 23:20.

28 BEFORE HEROD AGRIPPA II

196   *Herod the Great, who had tried to find*: Matthew 2:16-18.

199   *I was a Pharisee*: Philippians 3:4-6.

200   *Through all of this I have known*: Luke 24:44-49.

30 ROME AT LAST

214   *Tell the people they hear*: Isaiah 6:9-10.

215   *He wrote several letters to churches*: During Paul's time in Rome, he wrote Philippians, Colossians, Philemon, Ephesians, 1 and 2 Timothy, and Titus.

215   *Remember Jesus Christ, Timothy*: 2 Timothy 2:8-13.

31 ON EARTH AS IT IS IN HEAVEN

217   *Though he did not accept Jesus*: Mark 3:21; John 7:5.

217   *James and Jesus' other brothers*: 1 Corinthians 9:1-5.

217   *James felt called by God to serve*: Galatians 2:9.

217   *The Scribes and Pharisees placed James*: Eusebius of Caesarea, "The Martyrdom of James, Who Was Called the Brother of the Lord," in *Church History* 2.23.

218   *Barnabas continued on as a missionary*: Acts 15:36-39.

218   *Paul mentioned Barnabas*: 1 Corinthians 9:6.

218   *Barnabas was martyred*: John Fleetwood, *The Life of our Blessed Lord and Savior Jesus Christ: And the Lives and Sufferings of His Holy Evangelists and Apostles* (New York: Miller, Orton & Co., 1857), 455.

218   *During Paul's imprisonment*: 2 Timothy 4:11.

218   *Peter also benefited*: 1 Peter 5:13.

218   *Titus, known for his diligence*: 2 Corinthians 7:6; 8:17.

218   *Paul charged him to strengthen*: Titus 1:5.

218   *Later, Titus took the gospel*: 2 Timothy 4:10.

218   *Timothy, Paul's dear son*: Philippians 1:1; Colossians 1:1; Philemon 1.

219   *Paul commended Timothy often*: Philippians 2:19-23.

219   *Early records suggest that Timothy*: Eusebius, *The History of the Church* 3.4 (AD 325).

219   *Luke stayed with Paul*: Colossians 4:14; 2 Timothy 4:11; Philemon 24.

219   *He also cared deeply*: Luke 1:1-4.

219   *Along with being a writer*: Robert Grigg, "Byzantine Credulity as an Impediment to Antiquarianism," *Gesta* 26, no. 1 (1987): 5-6.

219 *Some believe Luke was martyred*: Michael Walsh, ed., *Butler's Lives of the Saints* (New York: HarperCollins, 1991), 342.

219 *Onesimus and Philemon*: Philemon 13-14.

219 *Some historians believe Onesimus*: This position was expounded by Professor John Knox in 1935 in his little booklet titled *Philemon Among the Letters of Paul.*

219 *After John and Peter were arrested*: Galatians 2:9.

220 *Peter was crucified by Nero*: John 21:18-19.

220 *There he preached about Christ*: 1 Peter 5:13.

220 *Many Christ-followers were rounded up*: Tacitus, Annals xv. 44. 3-8.

220 *As for Paul, it seems his case*: 2 Timothy 4:16-17.

220 *He did not conceal the fact*: 2 Timothy 1:16-18.

221 *The resurrection of Jesus Christ*: Ephesians 1:18-23.

221 *Together they would be the church*: John 17:21; Ephesians 4:1-16.

221 *After the resurrection, Jesus' disciples*: Acts 12:2.

221 *People are saved by grace*: Ephesians 2:8-9.

221 *Historically, God calls to himself*: Exodus 33:3-5; Deuteronomy 9:6-13; Proverbs 1:24-31; Ezekiel 2:3-4.

222 *Christ died for the ungodly*: Romans 5:6-8.

222 *The message of the cross*: Colossians 2:13-14.

222 *The Holy Spirit, who attends*: Acts 2:16-21.

222 *Jesus promised that the Spirit*: John 4:23-24; Acts 7:48-51; John 14:15-17.

222 *The Holy Spirit illuminates*: 1 Peter 1:12.

222 *The Holy Spirit is the guarantee*: 2 Corinthians 1:21-22; 5:1-10; Romans 8:9-11; 8:23.

222 *God's people together as a single body*: Romans 12:3-8; 1 Corinthians 12:12-31.

222 *destroys the dividing walls*: 1 Corinthians 15:20-28, 42-49; Ephesians 2:11-16.

222 *Those who place their faith*: Ephesians 4:11-16.

222 *They are transformed*: 2 Corinthians 5:16-21; Colossians 3:10.

222   *made one by the finished work*: Ephesians 4:4-6.

222   *Together they walk*: Romans 6:3-5.

222   *living out their days in the community*: 1 Thessalonians 4:13-18.

222   *All who believe are one*: Galatians 3:28.

222   *Believers in Christ are those*: Ephesians 5:7-14; John 3:16-21; 12:35-36.

RETELLING THE STORY SERIES

The Retelling the Story series explores the narrative arc of the Bible in compelling language that is faithful to the text of Scripture. The stories are told to help readers hide God's Word in their hearts by way of their imaginations.

Also by Russ Ramsey

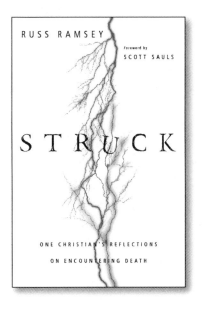

978-0-8308-4494-4